ANXIETY IN CHILDHOOD AND ADOLESCENCE:
ENCOURAGING SELF-HELP THROUGH
RELAXATION TRAINING

# ANXIETY IN CHILDHOOD AND ADOLESCENCE

ENCOURAGING SELF-HELP
THROUGH RELAXATION TRAINING

FRANK CARTER and PETER CHEESMAN

CROOM HELM
London ● New York ● Sydney

© 1988 Frank Carter and Peter Cheesman
Croom Helm Ltd, Provident House,
Burrell Row, Beckenham, Kent BR3 1AT

Croom Helm Australia, 44-50 Waterloo Road,
North Ryde, 2113, New South Wales

Published in the USA by
Croom Helm
in association with Methuen, Inc.
29 West 35th Street
New York, NY 10001

British Library Cataloguing in Publication Data
Carter, Frank
    Anxiety in childhood and adolescence:
    encouraging self-help through relaxation training.
    1. Anxiety in children 2. Child
    psychotherapy 3. Relaxation
    I. Title II. Cheesman, P.L.
    618.92′85233′0651    RJ506.A58

ISBN 0-7099-4806-9
ISBN 0-7099-4846-8 Pbk

Library of Congress Cataloging-in-Publication Data

ISBN 0-7099-4806-9
    0-7099-4846-8 (Pbk)

Printed and bound in Great Britain
by Billing & Sons Limited, Worcester.

# Contents

# Introduction

This book is written principally for parents and professionals in a position to help children and young people. It is unashamedly optimistic — a book about anxiety and what can be done about it, namely relaxation training.

The chapters follow a sequence which encourages the reader to become involved in the relaxation process, then to give serious thought to the nature of tension and relaxation, before undertaking to teach a relaxation technique to anyone else.

So the book actually opens with a chapter which provides direction through several relaxation exercises — clearly relaxation is an active not a passive process.

There then appear three chapters which consider what psychological tension is, its escalation into what is recognised as anxiety, and the concept of relaxation as being quite incompatible with anxiety. Relaxation, moreover, can be taught.

Chapters 5 and 6 look at various applications with regard to children, pressing the point that relaxation training is both an educational and a therapeutic aid. The exploratory work with cerebral palsied children has implications for all.

Having presented the case that tension in its extreme forms and whatever its source is indeed manageable — with relaxation as the key — we then present a short section of two chapters raising a number of theoretical considerations. Why and how relaxation training 'works' can be explained, but warrants further research.

The final chapter presents a model for teaching a child how to relax. It also offers a different technique from that provided in the first chapter. What is anticipated is that the informed reader will be able to make selections and modifications appropriate to the needs of the child.

Since the 1930s when Jacobsen formalised relaxation training as a means of achieving control over one's phobias, the subject has interested clinicians and developed in many forms. But it has gained somewhat grudging respectability, despite, or perhaps because of, its very simplicity of concept, its lack of mystique and its sheer practicality. To learn relaxation skills requires little more than awareness and motivation, opportunity and commitment. To teach them demands knowledge of the techniques involved, patience and sympathy with the learner.

Applications of relaxation training have been diverse: parachutists in training, to relax in order to master the fear of jumping from an aircraft; expectant mothers, to control their breathing and abdominal muscles preparatory to going into labour; and increasingly, courses in business management teach relaxation skills to cope with the stress of industrial relations. But these are select fields and concern the adult population only.

The subject of children, however, tends to concern everyone. Children happy and contented with their lot, children learning well and coping well with whatever life throws at them, children assured and at ease in the relationships they form and maintain, children contributing to the quality of life — such are the aims of parents and those who care for children generally.

The following chapters recognise the applicability of relaxation training to children. The authors describe relaxation as an invaluable aid to children in combating anxiety and extremes of tension, encountered in a wide range of different situations. Relaxation techniques can be taught and the application of relaxation training helps children grow in confidence in dealing with difficult situations.

Children as well as adults do meet stressful circumstances daily. Those who care for and work with children of all ages need to be aware of this, and to develop their own skills so as to become better managers of their own anxieties and those facing their children.

Children who should benefit as a result of this book are no select population. They are not a clearly defined class or group singled out in some way for our attention. The book considers all children who need at some time to cope with the demands of living. Such demands are recognisably 'normal', but to the child without a coping strategy, they can provoke a level of anxiety which makes coping all the more difficult. The child's behaviour is then perceived as a 'problem' by the adult, who is in turn at a loss to know how best to deal with a worsening situation.

So difficulties create probems and problems create anxiety. Anxiety then merely aggravates the problem. No-one, neither child nor parent nor the person who is *in loco parentis*, knows what to deal with — the problem or the anxiety caused by it! Such anxiety spirals and disables. This effect is repeatedly referred to or described in the text. But parents and others are also given ideas about how to recognise anxiety in children, and are provided with a means to enable them to cope.

For if we do not recognise anxiety, or if we perceive it as something different, then we are likely to interpret matters in an unhelpful fashion. The likely solution will be unconstructive, the outcome for child and adult alike negative rather than positive.

But the adult or child who is alive to the anxiety component in any given situation is, at the very least, given a chance to tackle it constructively. This constructive option becomes available to someone who has learned how to relax and how to apply that training when necessary. Relaxation training not only reduces tension, it puts the subject back in control. Instead of being overwhelmed or overwrought you have a means at your disposal whereby you can take whatever positive action you deem necessary. For the child, the very realisation that he can in fact improve matters which otherwise would certainly deteriorate, is immensely reassuring and awakens a great range of possibilities. Social and educational opportunities now open up, and indeed the very ability to learn is enhanced.

In those cases where the child's influence over the environment is severely restricted, the caring adult can act so as to give greater control to the child. Examples quoted in the text include the authors' experience with cerebral palsied children, who are described in terms of their muscle tensions, and for whom there is evidence and hope that even such chronic disabling effects may be rendered more manageable through relaxation training.

Due regard is paid to individual differences. Certainly some children are more amenable than others to relaxation training. Some more than others are able to apply it when faced with real-life difficulties. Some experience anxieties frequently, some hardly at all. By the same token, those in care of children vary in their readiness to recognise and respond appropriately to their needs. So we argue for relaxation training and its far-reaching application. If it is part of a child's armoury then it can be employed whenever necessary.

Every attempt is made to encourage and to maintain throughout this book a vein of optimism when dealing with children and the anxiety they face. Accordingly, what now follows is aimed at children and young people, as well as parents and the teaching and helping professions, in the expectation that all can bring relaxation training to bear wherever needed.

*Authors' note*:
As a mode of convenience only, throughout this text: the 'child' will normally be referred to by the pronoun 'he'; the 'adult' by the pronoun 'she'; and the term 'child(ren)' should be taken to refer to young person(s) of school age.

# 1

## Learning How to Relax

*The contents of this chapter are useful in their own right.
Moreover, anyone who has become familiar with 'how to relax'
will have a keener appreciation of the chapters to follow.*

Let us start with learning a relaxation technique.

You, the reader, are addressed in this chapter and encouraged to
be guided by the ideas which follow — if you wish to become profi-
cient in relaxing yourself, and/or help develop useful relaxation skills
in others. In due course you will learn to adopt a more relaxed strategy
in coping with your own concerns — including the concern you have
about your own child or children for whom you are responsible. You
will help children to relax if you yourself are more relaxed to begin
with.

Your first priority in developing skills is to create optimum conditions
whereby effective learning can take place.

Although attention will be given to transferring the learned skills
to those situations where they are most needed, initially relaxation
training can best take place in the quiet seclusion of your own home.
Make a point of setting aside a fixed time every day over a period
of say, 1½–2 weeks, when you can be alone and undisturbed. Choose
a room free from distractions. Make sure none of your clothing is
restrictive, but allows you full freedom of movement. Give yourself
enough arm room and floor space, so that you are not impeded from
stretching out fully in all directions, and have handy a comfortable,
but firm, hard-backed chair.

Also to hand it is advisable to have a standard cassette-recorder.
If the notes which follow are pre-recorded, you will find it easier to
engage in the exercises, freed from having to read as you go along.
The recorded voice should be soothing as well as clear in pitch and
tone, and needs to inspire confidence in the listener.

So much is obvious. Remember that, as well as what you do at
home, you should get into the way of practising your relaxation

exercises at odd moments throughout the day. Accordingly, the exercises are arranged in sets: those which you can undertake while sitting down, some for when you are standing, and others when you are able to lie and stretch out. Some you can do in any position.

Each exercise takes the form of a stretching or a tensing of certain muscles, followed by relaxing the same muscles. If, by tensing any area of the body, you feel pain, or the muscles remain tensed or tend to spasm, you should forgo the tensing stage and concentrate only on relaxing the area concerned. No exercise is intended to do more than produce a degree of tension compatible with your own individual limits of what is comfortable, but clearly you must profit from the exercise. Repeatedly, you are asked to take each exercise to whatever point is necessary to enable you to distinguish between feeling tense and feeling relaxed.

You are also advised to work to your own plan. Some may complete all three sets of exercises in sequence; others may prefer a break between them. Depending on the time you allow between the exercises or sets, you may complete the programme in anything from ½ hour to 1½ hours. Eventually you should select according to need; do not skimp but spend plenty of time in the early stages to master what may at first seem a misleadingly simple repertoire.

Throughout the three sets the language is similar, so as to consolidate previous learning while exercising the same or adjacent muscle groups. This allows you options when wishing to exercise during the day.

The suggested images are often similar too. The idea of the image is to provide yourself with some picture, the more remote from reality the better, which will help you associate any tension you experience at any time, with a relaxed response. Peter Russell, in *The brain book* (1979), describes how invoking images can aid recollection — the memory then serves to consolidate the learning as it takes place.

You might like to think of your own images, to encourage you to day-dream your way through the exercises! So you will learn to use your day-dreams as an aid to relaxation. While, for some, an image cannot easily be conjured up, and for others it is not needed, if imagery helps *you*, use it. The images should not in any way restrict or inhibit, but should serve as cues to the relaxation process. Encourage the child you are teaching to develop his own images, and through them establish reliable cues.

## A. SITTING EXERCISES

### 1. Sitting posture

*Suggested image*: you are king of the castle; you are in control, perfectly calm, governed by reason and governing reasonably; only when you are ready will you move, and do what you consider needs doing.

Sit with your back against the upright of the chair, so that you are not slouching at all. Put your hands down by your sides and under your buttocks, so that you are seated on the palms of your hands. In this position your fingers should feel two bones as your body weight presses down on to your hands. These are known as your 'sitting bones'. Remove your hands. Whenever you sit you should consciously try to ensure that both these bones are in contact with the seat of your chair.

With your back against the upright of the chair and your bottom set firmly on the seat, now plant your two feet about a shoulder's width apart, on the floor immediately in front of the chair. The soles and heels of your feet should both be in contact with the floor.

Rest both wrists on top of your thighs, so that your slightly bent fingers almost reach your knees.

In this position your body is well set to begin to relax thoroughly; and if this is an unfamilar position for you to hold for any length of time, nevertheless persevere with it. Remind yourself periodically throughout the day to adopt *this* sitting posture rather than the sideways slouch, the cross-legged perch, etc.

### 2. Deep breathing

*Suggested image*: now you are sitting on a cloud; when you inhale, the fresh breezes fill the cloud to bursting point, providing you with a platform of buoyancy and self-confidence; exhale, and take a well-earned rest as the pillow deflates.

Place one hand on your stomach. Inhale fully and, as you do so, feel your stomach rise (not flatten); your hand registers the movement outwards. Hold one full breath for some five seconds and then exhale slowly. As you breathe out, so your tummy flattens; now your hand registers the movement downwards and inwards.

An additional guide to you that you are breathing in a relaxed fashion is that, as you inhale and your stomach rises, so the small of your back leaves the upright of the chair. As you exhale you again feel contact between the small of your back and the back of the chair.

Practise breathing in and out in this manner for five or six full breaths. For all the exercises which follow, try to maintain a steady, even breathing rhythm.

## 3. Hands and arms

*Suggested image*: you have to repeatedly stop yourself from falling over a cliff edge; finally you are safe and can breathe easy.

Lift your hands off your thighs a few inches, clench your fists as tightly as possible for five seconds. Feel the tension in your fists and lower arms, unclench them and allow them to fall back on to your thighs and relax thoroughly. Experience the relief of all that tension leaving your hands and lower arms.

Check sitting position and breathing rhythm.

When you are ready, bend both arms to try to place the back of each hand on its respective shoulder (back of right hand on right shoulder, etc.). The top side of your lower arm should almost touch the bicep of that same arm. Hold for five seconds and feel the tension in biceps and cocked wrists. Relax, let both hands come to rest again on your thighs. Enjoy the sensation of relief as the tension ebbs out of arms and hands.

Check your sitting and breathing.

When ready, stretch both arms straight ahead at shoulder height, keeping them a shoulder's width apart. Stretch as far as you can. Note the strain in lower and upper arm. Hold this position for five or six seconds. Relax; once more allow your arms to drop by your side, elbows tucked in and wrists resting on your thighs.

Sit quietly, breathing comfortably, eyes closed if you prefer it that way, and reflect on the feelings you have just experienced. Note the difference between feeling tense and feeling relaxed.

## 4. Neck and shoulders

*Suggested image*: you are a child climbing up the inside of a

7

chimney; you are hemmed in on all sides; at last you pop your head out of the top; you look all around, surveying the whole world.

Hunch your shoulders as high as you can, so that they almost touch your ears. Feel the strain in your sides, shoulders and neck. Hold for five or six seconds, then relax, letting your shoulders droop. But maintain contact between your back and the upright of the chair. Rest your lower arms, wrists and hands on your thighs.

Now stretch the neck muscles in harmony with your breathing rhythm. As you breathe in, concentrate your gaze straight ahead; then as you exhale, turn your head at right angles so that your chin is over your right shoulder. Hold that position for a few seconds then face front again, inhaling as you do so. Exhale when turning this time to the left. Repeat several times to right and left, breathing fully and evenly as you go.

Again, from the eyes-front position, inhale deeply. As you exhale look down, tucking the chin tight into your chest. Repeat several times.

Eyes-front, inhale. And as you breathe out, push your head as far back as it will go so that the back of your head touches between the shoulder blades. Repeat.

Now relax all the muscles you have just been stretching, flopping your head this way and that. Note the difference between tension and relaxation in those muscles.

## 5. The face

*Suggested image*: your entire face is a pool of water; as you wrinkle your eyes, tense your jaw, etc., you cause ripples on the water's surface; but you can disperse all ripples leaving the pool perfectly calm and undisturbed.

Concentrate on your eyes; close them very tightly for six or seven seconds. Relax; feel the tension begin to evaporate from around the eyes.

Now assume the surprised stare. Open your eyes as wide as you can, stretching the forehead upwards. Hold for a count of seven. Then relax all those muscles you have just stretched around the eyes and forehead; let your eyes gently close.

Imagine the most peaceful scene. Bask in the comfort of relaxation; compare it with the ache of the tension you have been experiencing.

Give your attention to your mouth. Begin by pressing your lips tightly together, forcing them shut, allowing nothing to enter or leave. Hold for several seconds. Relax, parting your lips slightly. Feel them tingle, let your eyelids fall, and have a rest.

Check your sitting and breathing.

Think of your tongue. Concentrate on pressing the tip of your tongue into the roof of your mouth. Note the strain on tongue and in lower jaw. Hold. Relax, allowing your tongue to find repose at the bottom of your mouth.

Finally, clench teeth, setting your jaw as determinedly as possible. Hold for as long as you are able, up to ten seconds. Relax, close your eyes, let your jaw hang loose and enjoy release from all that tension. Take your time before continuing.

## 6. Feet and legs

*Suggested image*: your legs form a bridge which people must cross to safety; as the numbers on the bridge increase so does the strain; first one bridge support then the other takes the strain; but at length all get across to the peace and safety of the other side.

Check your breathing and your sitting posture.

Stretch your legs straight out parallel to the floor. Point toes and keep both legs steady, about a shoulder's width apart. Hold for up to ten seconds. Note where you feel tensions. Relax, letting your feet fall to the floor. Draw your feet back towards the chair as you resettle into your sitting posture.

Now, taking one leg at a time, grasp the left leg on the shin just below the knee and gently pull it up, towards and across your chest until you feel the strain. Hold for ten to 15 seconds. Repeat with the right leg. Relax, and settle back into your sitting posture.

## 7. Rest and review

As before, take stock of what you have been doing. Note the tension you have induced and the relaxation response you have been able to bring into effect. Give some thought to how and when, throughout the day, you might practise some or all of these exercises. In your mind's eye try to build associations between familiar daily occurrences and these images or something similarly far-fetched — e.g. associate sitting down to lunch with sitting on your cloud — and learn to relax

9

when eating. Continually check posture and breathing, especially when pressure looms. At most moments of stress, at least you will be able to clench and release your fists or stretch your legs. Simply — learn to relax when sitting.

## B. STANDING EXERCISES

### 1. Standing posture

*Suggested image*: like the Statue of Liberty you stand tall and assertive; you are dependable and aware, taking in all you see around you.

Legs apart, stand with your weight equally balanced between both feet. Allow arms and hands to hang by your sides. Straighten your back and lift your chin. Sway gently from side to side, just enough to let first one heel then the other lift a fraction off the floor. Without taking either foot off the floor entirely, swing easily for ten seconds or so. Now stop and feel how loose-limbed you are, yet with both feet firmly planted on the ground. Finally, you may like to rehearse some of the exercises you managed from the sitting position, selecting from the face, neck and shoulder stretches.

### 2. Deep breathing

*Suggested image*: buffeted by the swell of the sea and the force of the gale, you stand firm; you are not distressed but remain calm.

In the standing position, again pay particular attention to how you breathe. As you inhale place one hand on your stomach. Hand and stomach should rise together as the air inflates your lungs. Breathe out and your hand drops as your stomach flattens. Notice the rolling sensation as your stomach rises when you breathe in, and flattens again when you breathe out. Practise this whenever you adopt your standing posture.

Every now and then you might also practise a stomach-hardening exercise. Inhale fully, to the extent that your stomach hardens — as though in anticipation of a punch. Hold the stomach muscles taut for five or six seconds before releasing. Allow the air to escape and the stomach to relax again.

### 3. Legs and lower back

*Suggested image*: you are required to carry a weight on your back; but you can bear the strain and, by degrees, do so with comfort and ease.

Checking your posture, feet planted a shoulder's width apart, breathing steady and rhythmical, go into a stretch as follows. Lean the upper body forward from the hips, aiming to touch the floor with your fingers. Do not at this stage attempt to keep your knees locked and your legs straight, but merely bend forward, legs more or less upright, while your body stretches from midriff down to the floor. Hang in this position for a few moments, breathing easily.

Now tighten the leg muscles, just a fraction. Fingers maintaining contact with the floor, begin to straighten your legs, stretching until you feel tension in the backs of your legs. At this point hold the stretch for some five or six seconds.

Relax, letting your knees buckle slightly again, and resume the hanging position. Slowly curl upwards into your standing posture. Take a few deep breaths and repeat the whole exercise twice.

### 4. Trunk and upper limbs

*Suggested image*: you are taking off, trying to fly; you have to work at it, spreading your wings in various positions — until you are flying with ease.

Check posture and breathing. Inhale deeply, and as you breathe out stretch your arms straight out in front of you. Stretch arms, hands and fingers. Reach as far out as you can. Hold the stretch for up to eight seconds, noting the tension in shoulders and arms. Relax, letting your arms drop by your sides. Again feel the difference between tension and relaxation.

Repeat the exercise, this time pushing your arms and hands straight out to the sides, into the crucifix position. Hold for eight seconds or so. Relax, letting your arms drop. Note the difference between tension and relaxation.

Repeat, and now thrust your arms high above your head. Reach and hold the stretch, noting where you feel tension. Relax, but leave your arms aloft and clasp your hands, interlocking the fingers. Feet apart, pull your hands first to the left then to the right. In this way you stretch sideways from the waist. Repeat several times left and right.

## 5. Rest and review

Finally, stand easy and relaxed, eyes closed. Breathe fully and rhythmically. Quite composed and comfortable, take note once more of the difference between tension and relaxation in the various parts of the body.

Again, consider how you might make use of relaxation exercises and relaxing imagery in the course of your day. How often do you find yourself standing? When listening to someone or watching something, or waiting in a queue, give a moment's thought to posture. Picture yourself holding this posture.

Imagine yourself on your feet, being harassed, then go into your deep-breathing routine, keeping yourself alert and calm. Get into a habit: as often as you are in a standing position, use it to relax.

## C. LYING DOWN EXERCISES

## 1. Lying posture

*Suggested image*: think of yourself as a ship at sea; you are safe and secure and know what course you are on.

Again, many of the exercises you undertook from standing or sitting positions can be practised when lying down. The best surface is a well-carpeted floor, for you need a base that is firm but comfortable. For suitable working space you want the length of your body plus your arm length, plus approximately three times the width of your body.

Lie flat back on the floor, arms and legs tucked in. Feel the floor with your shoulders and elbows, buttocks and heels. Head still, look straight above. Check that your breathing is regular and full, and that your arms are resting easily by your sides, palms down on the floor.

Now bend your knees, pointing them to the ceiling and pulling your heels up to about nine inches from your bottom. Lie still, eyes closed. Relax and enjoy your lying posture.

## 2. Deep breathing

*Suggested image*: the ship again — you can feel the swell of the sea and, while you sense possible and actual dangers all around, you know you can prevent panic and encourage calm; you are in control.

Place one hand on your stomach and inhale. Your hand rises as your stomach does. As you breathe out, your hand and stomach flatten. Note that when you breathe in, the small of your back leaves the floor; breathe out and the small of your back once more descends to touch the floor. Recognize this rolling motion and practise it.

Occasionally, tighten the stomach muscles as though someone were about to jump on top of you. Inhale, then hold your breath for five seconds before exhaling slowly and completely. Concentrate on breathing, tightening the tummy muscles and relaxing them.

## 3. Lower limbs

*Suggested image*: you are a footbridge across a ravine, thrust from side to side in the gale; everyone depends on you for a safe crossing; and you withstand all pressures, proving solid, secure and trustworthy.

Check posture and breathing. Knees bent and touching, inhale and, as you exhale, swing your knees together down to touch the floor on the right. Inhale and swing back to the vertical position. Breathe out, and this time swing knees together down to the left.

Describe this arc from one side to the other, knees bent and touching, several times — inhaling and exhaling rhythmically as you do so. Note the stretch and tension in the upper thighs and round your hips. Repeat as often as you can without discomfort. Relax and again note the difference between relaxation and tension.

This stretch is assisted and developed if you roll your head from side to side, at the same time as you swing your knees down to the floor — but in the opposite direction. Thus, as you swing knees to the right, turn your head fully to the left. Repeat — knees now to the left, head to the right — and so on. You can practise moving rhythmically, producing a full body twist with each full breath. Just move unhurriedly, breathe deeply and stretch fully. And relax.

Now stretch your legs down on to the floor, pointing your toes as far as they can reach. Stretch and hold for five or six seconds. Relax. Take this exercise a stage further: as you point your toes, tighten your buttocks; stretch your legs and arch your back off the floor. Your weight should now be supported only by shoulders, elbows and heels — and if you can, only by shoulders and heels for a few moments. Feel the stretch the length of your body. Hold for five or six seconds.

Relax, bend your knees and resume the lying posture. Think of the difference, and where you have felt it, between tension and relaxation.

## 4. Midriff area

*Suggested image*: you are trapped beneath a pile of rubble; but your arms come free to straighten and push against the weight; the more you can straighten your back the more weight rolls off your back, and away from your lower limbs; at last you have pushed yourself free and you can breathe easy.

Roll flat on to your front. Keep your legs together and toes pointed downwards. Bend your arms and spread your hands on either side of your head, with palms down on the floor; the heel of each hand should be on the floor underneath its corresponding shoulder. You are about to do an upper-body stretch from the press-up position.

Check your breathing. Note that when you inhale you are pressing hard on to the floor. As you breathe out you will feel really relaxed all over.

Hands under shoulders, push only your upper body off the floor, gradually straightening your arms, or as nearly as you can. Meanwhile, you must make every effort to keep your legs and hips in contact with the floor. The effect is that you stretch the muscles at the base of the spine and you become aware of stretching in the abdominal region; you push your back up towards the vertical position, whilst maintaining the horizontal from toes to hips. When you feel the overall stretch, hold it for a few seconds only. Relax, bending your arms again. Practise this exercise three or four times, exhaling as you push your trunk off the floor.

## 5. Rest and review

Roll on to your back again. To conclude this series of tensing and relaxing, have a good long stretch. Extend your entire body as long as it will go, arms along the floor above your head, and legs and toes stretching far down from your trunk. Hold for several seconds before relaxing all the muscles.

Slip into the lying posture, knees bent and arms as before, by your sides. Close your eyes and again contemplate the difference between feeling tense and feeling relaxed.

As a final reminder to yourself, try the following. From the lying posture, turn your ankles inwards so that the soles of your feet touch and your knees spread apart. Bring your heels as close as you can to your bottom and allow your knees to fall apart as far as possible. You will feel the muscles inside your thighs and groin stretch, but do not force the stretch to the point of discomfort. You will find that this tenses the muscles in the upper leg area, but the rest of your body will be quite relaxed. Hold this stretch for as long as possible, recollecting all you have been doing in the way of relaxation exercises.

Once more, try to plan how you may fit relaxation into your daily schedule. Use whatever images help you.

With experience of this kind of tensing-and-relaxing, you grow sensitive to (feelings of) tension in this or that group of muscles. Then once the area of tension is identified, you will be able to concentrate on relaxing that area only. Learn to react habitually to tension whenever/wherever you feel it, by relaxing. In time you will not have to induce a consciously contrived tension, but will have available and ready a relaxed response to tension or to anything likely to cause tension. In other words, you will be able to do without a 'deliberate' cue.

# 2

## How Tension Develops

*In this chapter some consideration is given to the various environmental factors which are involved in the development of tension. Three such factors are identified — the physical environment, the social environment and the personal environment.*

In common with all other living creatures a child is affected by the environment in which he lives. For some simple forms of life this environment may be relatively unchanging and stable, and largely beyond the control of the organism. In contrast, a child may experience a whole variety of differing environments during the course of a day, some of which he may already know well, others which may be quite new to him. Compared with an adult, a child is frequently encountering situations of which he knows nothing, or where his information is incomplete and often distorted. The delightfully humorous incidents recounted by parents concerning their children will often have their roots in childish misconceptions of language or situation. It is useful to bear in mind that these misconceptions which amuse the parents represent a true reflection of reality for the child. The child's discovery of his failure to understand a situation will have the positive effect of contributing to his knowledge of the environment in which he lives, but must also reinforce a growing awareness of its uncertainty and unpredictability. This, in turn, can in certain circumstances lead to feelings of anxiety becoming associated with specific situations. It may also lead to a perception of all new situations as being potential sources of fear and anxiety.

Consider, for example, the experience of a child going to a swimming pool for the first time. It is fairly certain that he will have some expectations regarding what he is about to experience. He may have some idea of what swimming is; he will certainly know something of the nature of water; he will probably associate the word 'bath' with a whole variety of sensations, some of which are pleasant and a few, like having soap in his eyes, which are unpleasant. Unfortunately, none of these preconceptions are likely to do much to prepare him for the reality of that vast expanse of water, that strange smell, that echoing noise, the disorientation of being out of contact with the ground, and a whole host of other experiences which he may find overwhelmingly different from anything he has come across before. This is not to suggest that all children are necessarily going to find their first visit to a swimming pool something akin to a nightmare, but it is evident that the likelihood of the association of anxiety with this experience is very high. Many parents will agree that however well they have prepared their child for the event some anxiety will have arisen, and it is by no means unusual to find the level of this anxiety to be extreme to the point of hysteria. These sensations of anxiety may often be carried over into adult life where, in spite of the application of reason and logic to a situation now well understood, the fear remains. Even where the adult has learnt to swim it is still quite common for a *frisson* of anxiety to be experienced every time a swimming pool is entered or a large expanse of water observed.

Other situations with great potential for giving rise to anxiety are quite common in the everyday life of children because so much is still new to them. Perhaps paramount amongst these experiences which all children share is that of going to school. In this case the child is likely to have received a great deal of information about what school holds in store for him. Parents, brothers and sisters, playmates, books and television may all have contributed in raising a whole range of expectations which the child will carry with him to face this new experience. As with the swimming pool, the reality is likely to bear very little resemblance to the imagined concept that the child has constructed. The potential for raising anxiety inherent in this situation will vary greatly, and will be affected by a whole variety of factors including the nature of the school experience and how this departs from, or is congruent with, the child's expectations.

The two examples of the swimming pool and the school have been given in an attempt to illustrate how the environment can give rise to anxiety and thenceforward continue to be associated with feelings of tension beyond the time when logic would demand that such feelings should no longer be experienced. Many parents will recognise the feeling of hopelessness that accompanies attempts to use reason and logic to explain to a child that his fears about a particular situation are groundless. It is the child's perception of reality which is overriding and of central importance in determining his emotional response.

Important elements in the development of tension and anxiety are unpredictability and uncertainty. These could arise from the conviction that the events which occur conform to no order, they happen in a haphazard manner, they are random. To illustrate the tension-provoking nature of a random environment consider this example:

You are obliged to spend some time in a particular room every day for some years. The room looks perfectly ordinary and contains all the equipment that you require to carry out a range of tasks which you must complete because this is the custom and you have no choice in the matter. On some days when you go into the room you are able to carry out your tasks with no interference, but on another day you may pick up the object upon which you were working the day before but this time you receive a painful electric shock. That may be the only electric shock you receive that day but, on the other hand, you may receive six more. The next day all the things which had shocked you have resumed their innocence, but other objects which had previously been harmless have now become dangerous. Such an environment would only be predictable in its unpredictability. The random nature of this environment would undeniably lead to the development of anxiety and the experience of a state of tension whenever the time approached for the obligatory daily session in the room.

This extreme example would be equally anxiety-provoking for adults and for children, although perhaps the latter could claim that it bears a greater resemblance to their daily experience than it does for adults!

Children will also develop a whole range of expectations arising from their contact with those adults and children who form another major aspect of their environment. In the early years of childhood the closest contact will come from their parents and their brothers and sisters, but these contacts soon expand to include neighbours, nursery groups, school fellows, teachers and so on. A child will quite soon find himself within a complex structure of social relationships where he is obliged to try to make sense of a great variety of messages which come his way inherent in the actions and attitudes of those around him. If a child comes from a family background where he has learnt to expect to be treated calmly and considerately, where reasoned discussion is valued and aggressive behaviour is discouraged, he is likely to receive a rather rude shock on first being left at a nursery or playgroup. He will certainly experience difficulty in communicating with some of his fellow pupils just as some of these will find that he does not fulfil their expectations. It is, perhaps, surprising that so many children manage to adapt to these quite extreme changes in their social environments after an initial period of anxiety.

There is a well-established view held amongst many of those who have studied early childhood that the child sees himself as the centre of his world, and that the events which occur in that world come about as a consequence of his own thoughts or actions. This view is put forward most persuasively by Piaget (1929) and Piaget and Inhelder (1969). It can be thought of as an extreme form of self-centredness and as such it is given the special descriptive term 'egocentricity'. This egocentricity gradually decreases as maturation proceeds but at the time when children commonly make their initial contacts with groups outside their immediate family, it is still a potent aspect of the way in which they perceive their world. If this theoretical view is valid then the child experiencing contact with a relatively hostile and unpredictable environment is not only going to receive the aforementioned rude shock but may also believe himself to be in some way responsible for causing it!

A further complication lies in the great influence that imitative behaviour has during the early years of childhood. One possible response of a child finding himself in a strange and seemingly hostile environment is to take on aspects of this by imitation. This may have the effect of reducing his own worrying uniqueness within the group and making him feel more comfortable. A very comprehensive account of imitative learning may be found in Bandura and Walters (1964) and Bandura (1977). However, it is also likely that the production of this newly acquired behaviour at home will produce unexpected, and probably negative, responses from his parents. Once again the child finds himself in a potentially anxiety-provoking situation where the same behaviour gives rise to diametrically opposed effects according to where it is produced. Many parents will deal with these problems very effectively but, unfortunately, sometimes the problems go unrecognised, or if recognised, they are dealt with inappropriately. Anxiety about forming relationships with other children can arise because in some way these may be seen as posing a threat to the more crucial relationships with parents.

Uncertainty regarding the outcome of relationships with children or adults outside the close family group may lead to a variety of anxiety-related responses. The painfully shy child who shrinks from new contacts might well have experienced unfulfilled expectations regarding the behaviour of others, or had his own behaviour rejected or misunderstood. The child whose customary response when faced with a new situation is to act in an aggressive, precocious or over-familiar manner might well be responding to earlier experiences which have led to fear of the unknown and the over-reactive current behaviour may merely be a form of 'whistling in the dark'. Such a suggestion is lent credence by the transformation in the child which often follows a period of familiarisation with the new environment.

In this discussion of the way in which tension develops it is important to consider also the differences which exist between individual children. It would certainly be wrong to maintain that anxious responses to everyday situations arise only because of the past experiences children have met with in the external environment. Given very similar situations different children will react differently even if those children have had as nearly as possible the same upbringing. There are inherited factors which might be thought of as predispositions to produce certain patterns of behaviour. The realisation of these potentials may depend upon the experiences which impinge upon the child and their unique response to these.

An example may better illustrate this point. It is not at all unusual for certain families to acquire particular reputations in schools. These may range from expectations that all the children from one family will perform exceptionaly well in academic work to the expectation that as the parents and the other children from a family have been noted for their criminal activities then 'little Johnny' will also be a thief. The fact that these expectations have so often proved to be unfulfilled does not seem to have reduced the frequency with which they are made. There are, of course, many occasions when the predictions do come true, or at least seem to do so. Further examination of the evidence would cast some doubt even on the apparently obvious instances of environmental effects. The academically successful children do not all achieve to the same level, and hardly ever in the same fields. The rogues are rarely equally rougish and may express their roguery in widely differing ways! For a discussion of the way in which interaction occurs between a child's development and his educational experiences the reader might well refer to Donaldson, Grieve and Pratt (1983).

Where then have we got to in the consideration of the development of tension? Three fairly clear strands have been disentangled from the mass of experiences which confront a child. These strands are only separated to facilitate their discussion — in the real world they are inextricably interwoven. The first is the physical environment. The second is the social environment and the third is the child's own internal environment. Each of these will repay more detailed examination.

## THE PHYSICAL ENVIRONMENT

From a very early age children learn that their world consists of a great variety of different places. Whether they actually see these as separate entities or as a continuous succession of changing physical scenery is probably not important. What is important is that different activities are associated with these changing aspects of the environment. Consider first the home. Here the child will engage in play, in sleep, in eating, in toileting, in watching television and in many more pursuits. Some of these will lead to pleasure and to satisfaction, while others may lead to frustration or even to fear. These few examples by no means describe the whole gamut of feelings which will be experienced by the child at different times in the same physical environments. His bedroom may become associated with feelings of warmth and contentment, with the pleasure of experiencing loving parents reading to him and showing affection for him. However, he may also receive less positive messages. Irritation or even anger may be experienced if he has wet the bed; darkness may invest familiar objects with fearsome properties; even the contrast between the warm and comforting presence of a loved adult and being left alone may lead to feelings of rejection or abandonment. It can be appreciated that even for the child where bedtime is most meticulously managed so that his experiences are only good ones, there is little likelihood of this being achieved. It could even be argued that it would not be in the child's best interests for such perfection to be attained, as he will also need to learn about the less pleasurable feelings in order to acquire the means to deal with them. It is reasonable to suppose that the manner in which a child regards the onset of bedtime will depend on where his feelings lie on a scale ranging from pleasure to apprehension. In other words, if his positive feelings about bedtime outweigh the negative ones then he will look forward to the nightly ritual. If, on the other hand, his feelings are largely associated with fears of incurring the displeasure of his parents, or being left in the frightening darkness, bedtime for this child will be a time of anxiety and apprehension. These feelings, positive or negative or a combination of both, will come to be associated with the bedroom itself. The importance of not using the bedroom as a place of punishment becomes quite evident in the light of this discussion.

With this concept in mind of feelings becoming associated with different places it is instructive to observe the level of confidence with which a child approaches the various physical environments within the house. If there is evidence of anxiety it is worthwhile spending

21

some time in an attempt to analyse how it might have arisen. A common source of anxiety in many homes is the lavatory. For many children this represents the place above all others in the house where it is possible to learn how it feels to incur the disapproval of parents. To some workers with young children the successes and the failures of toilet training represent a major factor in the emotional development of the child, and the manner in which this will reach expression in adult life. Such an extreme approach will certainly not be put forward here, but it is likely that some of the techniques to be described later will be used to deal with anxiety which has aspects of its inception in too severe toilet training.

By no means all the contacts that the child makes in his home are under the control of adults. Some experiences will arise during the child's exploration of the environment, and some of these may be unpleasant. Children scald themselves, burn themselves, bruise and cut themselves all too frequently in the supposedly safe environment of the home. Providing the injuries are only slight these incidents can be helpful in teaching the child to view new situations with a degree of caution. If the injuries are severe it is not uncommon for a disabling fear of quite ordinary objects to stay with the victim into adult life. The tension caused by fear will often lead to clumsiness in handling the object of the fear, and a vicious circle is thus created which can only be broken if some active steps are taken to alleviate the tension.

There are other aspects of the physical environment which will impinge upon the child as he grows older. Shopping expeditions, visits to relations, outings to the park and, perhaps, to the swimming pool will all become associated with a variety of feelings some of which will only be fleeting, others of which may be intense. However, the next major set of environmental experiences are likely to be those associated with starting attendance at a nursery or at a school.

The possibilities which exist in this new set of circumstances are virtually limitless, and they will be the source of considerable examination throughout this work. For the moment, though, the concern will be solely for the physical aspects of the school environment. It is instructive to try to view the newly entered classroom from the point of view of the child. All those chairs, all those tables, the size of the room, all those toys, those tricycles, the playhouse, the climbing frame, the sandtray, water, slides . . . ! What reaction can be expected to such an Aladdin's cave of riches? What is expected of him? Can he play with all these things? Must he share them with these other children? Perhaps they are not for him at all.

It is not surprising that, for many children, school is a confusing and bewildering experience. For most the anxiety is short-lived, and going to school becomes an enjoyable experience to be looked forward to and appreciated. For some, the whole experience becomes invested with threat, and school remains for their entire academic career a place to be approached with apprehension. It is not at all unusual for a child who has been secure and happy in his primary school to develop feelings of anxiety on transferring to secondary education — feelings which may continue to mar his ability to benefit from his lessons throughout the remainder of his school life. However, the majority of children occupy a position between these two extremes of total acceptance and complete rejection. They will enjoy some lessons and dislike others. The classrooms where the enjoyable lessons take place will be associated with feelings of confidence and satisfaction. For some, the smells of the science laboratory will evoke feelings of hopelessness and failure, whilst for others the same smell may give rise to excitement. Any adult who has gone into a school for a meeting, or for some event concerning a child, will recognise the heavily evocative nature of its smells, its sights and its sounds. The link between the environment and emotions is very clear at such times, and for some adults there will be irrelevant feelings of anxiety associated with a time long past.

## THE SOCIAL ENVIRONMENT

In considering the social environment of the child it becomes clear that a very similar process of gradual expansion occurs to that which was described for the physical environment. For the first few weeks of life the baby is only conscious of the person directly in contact with him or within his very limited range of focused vision. He will learn to associate the presence of another person with the gratification of his desire for food or for comfort, and for some time it will not much matter who that person is as long as he or she satisfies the child's needs. However, even at this very early stage in the child's development there exist considerable possibilities for the building up of expectations regarding relationships with others. It is true that these expectations are concerned only with the satisfaction of basic needs such as food and general comfort. It is also true that at this stage these are of crucial importance to the child. He will learn to associate the feeling of being picked up with the satisfaction of his needs, with having his nappy changed (discomfort leading to comfort), with having

23

his hunger satisfied, with being bathed and with a general feeling of being handled.

It is possible for anxiety to arise even at this early age. For example, feeding does not always proceed with entire success. Sometimes there is insufficient milk or the mother's nipples are sore. Both of these conditions tend to lead to a feeling of tension in the mother which is easily transmitted to the baby accompanied by the discomfort of unsatisfied hunger. Bathtime, which for many children is a time of unalloyed delight, may yet produce feelings of tension if the child is not held securely. Sudden movements, especially if they lead to a loss of secure handling, sudden noises, sensations of excessive heat or of excessive cold can all lead to feelings of anxiety. That this has occurred will be shown by the child crying and struggling when confronted with situations where similar unwelcome things may happen. This might be expected, but what is less easy to predict is the further association of these unpleasant feelings with the person who was handling the child at the time. It is important that the adult involved should give immediate comfort to the child after such an occurrence in order to re-establish the association of positive feelings within the child towards them.

After a few months the baby will start to recognise the people within his social environment and to differentiate between his parents and other adults and between his brothers and sisters and his parents. This extension of his environment brings with it the possibility of a greater range of satisfactions beyond the gratification of physical needs. Play will become an important factor in the child's life, language will start to take on a degree of meaning, expression and gesture will comprise another vocabulary of social contact. The other people who inhabit the world of the child will still consist largely of his own family and he will learn to predict the outcomes of his interaction with them. Many of these outcomes will have positive and pleasurable connotations. He will associate his mother with food, with smiles, with outings and so on; his father may be associated with the excitement of being swung through the air; his brothers and sisters with play. It is, however, quite unlikely that this idyllic description will characterise all his relationships all the time. Sometimes his mother will be cross, his father impatient, his brother a tease and his sister will take away his toys. None of this should cause too much concern unless these negative aspects of his relationships come to outweigh the positive ones. Even more worrying for the child would be a state of unpredictability where an action one day produces a smile but the same action another day results in a frown, a shout or even a slap. Anxiety in children, even before they start school, is found quite frequently; and when it is there is usually a history of inconsistent treatment lurking in the background.

Starting school brings with it a whole range of new relationships with other adults and large numbers of other children. Frequently a group of children will start together in a nursery or a school and find themselves within a larger group that has been there for some time already. Adaptation to this new situation, which differs so vastly from the home, is by no means easy. The expectations which the child has developed regarding his contact with other children will be based upon the relationships which exist within his family group, although for some where there are no other children in the family, there will be little or no experience to apply to this strange situation. What is certain for all the new entrants is that they will be subjected to a range of different behaviours from other children well beyond anything which they have come across before. They may find themselves in a situation where they don't know what is expected of them amongst other children who clearly have knowledge presently denied to them.

The adults too, however gentle and kind, will differ from the child's parents — perhaps they may even give him his first experience of gentleness and kindness. It could well be that the child will for the first time come across a situation where he has to share the attention of an adult with other children, and where his demands have to be postponed whilst the needs of others receive priority treatment. The existence of these new factors in the environment does not necessarily lead to the development of tension and anxiety, but their potential for doing so should not be underestimated. If a child experiences problems in dealing with social interaction outside the family and he receives no help in overcoming these it is often the case that this will lead to a generalised inability to make satisfactory relationships throughout his life. A withdrawal into the family group, and an unwillingness to mix with other children or to go to school, is a common feature of tension arising from this source.

That the above sombre prediction only rarely comes true is largely a consequence of the strength and flexibility of the developing personality of the child. It is this personal environment to which the next section is addressed.


## THE PERSONAL ENVIRONMENT

This third factor in the environment of the child which needs to be taken into consideration is perhaps the most complex of all. It would be impossible to deal with all the rich variety of personality factors that give rise to the uniqueness of the individual. In any case this has been done many times elsewhere and not always with a great deal of agreement to be observed between the authors. It is, however, far too important an aspect of the child's environment to be ignored, and for this reason an attempt must be made to identify some of the factors which are central to the examination of the development of tension. These factors include the intellectual ability of the child, whether he is outgoing or introverted, dependent or independent, adaptable or rigid. Clearly there is already a wealth of individual differences possible even when consideration is limited to these few factors. Although they have been given as extreme positions which are directly opposite to each other, this is not meant to suggest that a child can only be, for instance, adaptable or rigid. He could, in fact, be anywhere along a continuum of which those states represent the extreme positions, and to make it still more complex, he could be at different positions along the continuum at different times. Add to this the further complexity of the various combinations and permutations which are possible between just these few factors and it becomes rather more obvious as to why agreement amongst authors who write about personality is somewhat rare!

Whilst accepting that it will not be possible to give a comprehensive account of the way in which personality factors relate to the development of tension, it is quite feasible to provide some illustrations of the possible interactions which might occur. The first factor mentioned was intellectual ability, and upon examining this a whole range of interactions which could be significant immediately become apparent. Firstly, it is important to make the point that the production of a global figure purporting to represent the intelligence level of a child has now been largely discredited. But it is also important to be aware that intellectual abilities do differ very widely, and that some of these can be usefully measured and used as a guide in designing a programme of work suited to the child's needs. Failure to do this will often lead to a child being faced with unrealistic demands which he cannot meet. Equally important is the need to ensure the strengths that a child possesses are recognised, for it can be as frustrating to be given no opportunity to do well as it is to be given too many opportunities to do badly. A child who never, or only rarely, experiences success will also most certainly become anxious about school. Personality is not a static, unchanging entity; it is susceptible to change in the light of experiences encountered. The constantly reinforced knowledge of failure which so many children experience in their schools contributes to the construction of a self-image of stupidity and ineptitude which may distort their whole experience of life. Fortunately, it is possible to alleviate some of the anxiety brought about by this, often quite inaccurate, self-image.

Although it would be an over-generalisation to state that outgoing children react better to school than introverted children there is a considerable element of truth in this. The shy, retiring child may often be happy at school and do well there, but this is usually as a consequence of his being handled in a sensitive and understanding way. The manner of the interaction between intellectual ability and introversion is often crucial. For example, a timid child who gains academic success, and because of this also gains the approval of his teachers, is far less likely to suffer from anxiety than a similarly timid child who also fails at his work. The first child may remain quite shy and retiring, but he will develop a level of confidence and self-esteem which will prevent his shyness from becoming crippling. In the latter case, however, the level of anxiety can reach a point where he becomes quite unable to face school at all.

Rigidity as an aspect of personality is likely to develop as a consequence of early insistence on very strict routines. This is often a very convenient way of bringing up a child, and has some features to commend it in that the child knows precisely what is expected of him. His treatment is completely consistent and he is not obliged to make decisions. Unfortunately, some of the consequences of such an upbringing are far from beneficial to the child. He will usually manage quite happily in the home but as soon as he is placed in a different environment he has no resources at his disposal to help him to adapt to the changed situation. Once again a probable result is the development of anxiety. An extreme, though maladroit, strategy sometimes adopted by a child to deal with this problem is to surround himself with a complicated ritual of trivial behaviours which presumably have the effect of restoring some sort of order into what he regards as a chaotic world. By retreating into this world of his own making he is able to reduce his anxiety temporarily until such time that the demands to join the real world become too powerful to be ignored and anxiety returns. The adaptable child may have had a much less structured upbringing, even a chaotic one, but whatever else he lacks he will be a past master at dealing with change!

At birth the baby is completely dependent upon others outside himself, and for many years a considerable degree of dependence remains. This is one of the most difficult aspects of child-rearing that parents must face. The initial dependence manifested by the child is often very satisfying to his mother, as it is to himself. The very survival of the child is the responsibility of his parents for quite a long period and it is not easy to accept that this position changes and the child needs to be helped towards achieving an appropriate degree of independence. Some children arrive at school without any preparation in independence training, unable to dress themselves, unable to wash themselves, unable to make decisions for themselves. Even the demands of a nursery class leave them bewildered and insecure. The most common reaction is to attempt to displace their need for dependence to their nursery teacher who is probably unable and unwilling to take on the role of the mother. A good teacher will embark upon a programme of independence training with the child in consultation with the mother but, unfortunately, there are some less able teachers who at one extreme attempt to adopt the role of the mother and at the other extreme leave the child to sort things out for himself as best he can. Some succeed, some fail, all experience a greater or lesser degree of anxiety.

## THE RESPONSE TO TENSION

In the previous sections of this chapter the various conditions which may have given rise to tension have been considered in some detail. The level of tension which occurs in response to similar situations can vary at different times within the same individual. Situations which give rise to extreme tension in one person may leave another virtually unaffected. The approach which is taken in this book regarding the development of tension is not markedly different from that which is adopted by many of those who work with anxious children or adults. It is accepted that the level of tension which develops is dependent upon a variety of factors, not the least of which is the past experience which an individual child brings to the current situation. This past experience will determine what kind of reaction will occur in response to the tension. The main thrust of the rest of this book is towards providing the child with a means of dealing with the tension in order to bring about an altered and, it is hoped, a more helpful response.

A few examples of the various reactions to tension which have been encountered in children will illustrate the central role of tension in providing a trigger for behaviour.

Jenny is a girl of 14 years of age who attends her local comprehensive school. She is considered to be a very pleasant, though rather dull child, who cannot read very well. Because of this she does poorly in academic subjects. Her parents are concerned about her failure to succeed at school as the rest of the family are bright. They are particularly concerned because in all respects where reading does not mediate the acquisition of knowledge Jenny seems to be very sharp indeed. Unfortunately, having provided some degree of remedial help, which proved to be ineffectual, the school has accepted that she is just a slow-learning child. Her parents are not prepared to give up so easily and they insist that she be seen by an educational psychologist — one of the authors.

He administers a variety of tests which do not require Jenny to make a written response or to carry out any reading, and it very soon becomes apparent that her parents are correct in their assumption that she is quite a bright girl. What also becomes apparent, after she is asked to read aloud a passage from a book, is that her level of tension increases to a remarkable degree. A confident, assured young girl suddenly becomes tense and withdrawn, hesitant in her speech and awkward in her manner. Her extreme state of anxiety renders her unable to employ the few reading skills she possesses, and what is even more unfortunate is that she confesses that whenever she is confronted with a reading task at school or at home, alone or with others, the same reaction occurs. The approach adopted to deal with her problem focuses primarily on reducing the level of tension engendered and thus controlling the anxiety.

Richard, who is ten years old, attends a special school for children with moderate learning difficulties where he copes quite well with the level of work required of him, but he gives rise to great concern because of his habit of making loud inconsequential noises. These also occur at home and when he is taken out shopping or to a restaurant. On investigating his early childhood experiences it is revealed that the family had moved between Spain and England a number of times during the time when Richard would have been involved in acquiring language. On each of these occasions the social environment became almost entirely Spanish or entirely English as the language adopted by the family reflected the country they were in at the time. This is because his mother is Spanish, and during the time they were in Spain the father was with them only for brief periods.

By the time Richard is encountered he has been permanently in England for some time and his language is English, although he understands some Spanish and occasionally hears it spoken by his mother and his elder sister. It is also evident that the shouting had started on the first occasion the family had moved from England to Spain, and had continued intermittently ever since. It is requested that careful records should be kept both at school and at home which will indicate the nature of the situation immediately prior to the shouting occurring. It is no surprise to learn that, without exception, the situations reported always contain some element which is new to Richard. He is highly susceptible to anything even slightly outside his normal routine and which disturbs the rather obsessively regular patterns of behaviour within which he feels most comfortable. The shouting response seems to be an echo of his past response to the confusion of language which surrounded him, and is his way of dealing with too much tension. Within a few weeks of being given another response which he could use when confronted with a potentially anxiety-provoking situation his shouting has completely disappeared.

Martin produces behaviour of a type with which many parents and teachers are only too familiar. He is a bright and engaging seven-year-old whose parents are becoming quite distracted by the fact that he is frequently the subject of complaints from school and from neighbours regarding his apparently uncontrollable rages. They can only concur with these reports because the same behaviour happens at home. He has a brother, 18 months younger than himself, with whom he enjoys a good relationship. His mother had experienced great difficulty at the younger child's birth and had been obliged to spend many months in hospital. No blame could attach to anyone for this crucial interruption in what had been a normal upbringing for Martin, but little imagination is required to appreciate the potential dangers that this situation held. Many different outcomes were possible but for Martin the response to tension is outwardly expressed aggression. He is aware of the feelings which build up prior to an eruption and he describes them as 'feeling as though I'm going to burst'. Giving him a new technique with which he could deal with these feelings produces an immediate reduction in the outbursts, and within a year they have ceased entirely.

With all these examples the children had learnt inappropriate responses to states of increasing tension. It was not that the tension was not being dealt with; in each case a reduction of the state of tension and a return to their form of normality was achieved. In the vast majority of cases children will develop a strategy for dealing with tension and, again, in the majority of cases these will be quite successful in keeping adults from worrying about them. However, even the successful strategies are frequently inappropriate or of limited value to the child, and could be replaced by techniques having wide general utility. In subsequent chapters it is intended not only to deal with these techniques but to offer some help to parents and others concerned with children to recognise tension and the signs of its development.

# 3

## Relaxation — the Other Side of Tension

*In this chapter the concept of the 'tension . . . relaxation' continuum is introduced. The monitoring of physiological arousal by biofeedback instruments is discussed, with some description given of those which might be used.*

The concept of tension, and the manner of its development, has been dealt with in some detail, and the view put forward is that tension can be experienced at distinctly different levels. It is further suggested that it is useful to consider the possibility of tension being reduced to a level where it is not experienced at all and where a different kind of experience, that of relaxation, takes over. This process can be likened to the sensation produced by temperature. A common experience is to enter a warm building having become very cold from exposure to a cutting wind. The outcome of this is not to change immediately from feeling cold to becoming comfortably warm, but for the cold to gradually dissipate until it is replaced by a sensation of warmth. It is conceivable that it would be possible to be aware of a level of sensation where the body was felt to be neither warm nor cold but at a point between the two. It is not too difficult to think of the sensation of body temperature as a continuous range of experiences with being much too cold at one extreme and much too hot at the other. There would be a whole range of feeling between the two extremes which could be described subjectively in a variety of ways in terms of temperature, of comfort and discomfort, or perspiring and shivering. Such a continuous range of steps along a single scale, e.g. temperature, a range of steps which could be infinite in number, is often referred to as a 'continuum'.

The same idea of the continuum is very useful in describing the states of tension and relaxation. It is possible to regard these as being, in fact, opposite levels of the *same* state. This is precisely the point of view being put forward here. An important aspect of this is that the state itself is regarded as being neutral in the same way as temperature is neutral. Temperature is not of itself concerned with perspiring or shivering, but is only associated with such sensations when other conditions pertain — e.g. being without a coat in cold weather or having engaged in vigorous exercise. It is just so with the single scale of tension and relaxation — the level at which it is being experienced will give rise to a whole variety of feelings. These might be positive feelings of pleasurable anticipation or contentment or negative feelings of fear or anger. Thus, 'tension . . . relaxation' is seen as being the precursor of emotion. At a high level of tension it is likely that feelings of anxiety would be experienced, whereas at the relaxation end of the continuum the emotions felt are likely to be those associated with contentment or placidity. A very important advantage accrues from adopting this view of the 'tension . . . relaxation' continuum as being of itself quite neutral. It is this: if, as is often the case, the word tension is loaded with negative connotations — anxiety, apprehension, stress — then it becomes difficult to accept that there may be positive aspects to certain levels of tension being experienced at appropriate times. For example, the level of tension of an athlete's body immediately prior to an event will cause a degree of anticipation and apprehension to be felt. This emotional state is beneficial to the production of optimum performance providing it is not too highly charged. Some athletes never seem to produce their best performances on the big occasions, and this is almost certainly as a result of their tensional state being too high, leading to over-apprehension and an apparent loss of form. Similarly, in other situations where optimum performance is sought — e.g. taking examinations, attending interviews, tackling complex problems — it is advantageous to experience a fairly high level of tension leading to appropriate emotional states. Equally, too high a level of tension resulting in anxiety being felt leads to those less desirable performances described variously as 'becoming tongue-tied', 'going to pieces', 'all fingers and thumbs'.

This relationship between the position on the 'tension . . . relaxation' continuum and the ability to carry out tasks efficiently is one of the most crucial concepts stated here, and as such merits some further expansion. The body is at one of its most relaxed levels when asleep. On first awakening the possibility of producing optimum physical or mental performance is considerably less than it will be after an hour or two have elapsed. The more aroused the body becomes, the better able it is to deal efficiently with the tasks undertaken. However, this is true only to a point. The body can become too aroused, too tense and at this point, instead of efficiency continuing to rise with an increase in tension, the opposite effect may be observed. For example, a typist under pressure to produce a document within very demanding time constraints may well find that she is making an uncharacteristic number of errors. An athlete reaching a pinnacle of achievement such as representing his country at the Olympic Games may make tactical mistakes which belie his experience of competition.

A considerable amount of research work has been carried out on this topic which it would not be appropriate to describe in detail here, but to which some reference must be made.

The 'tension . . . relaxation' continuum springs from the theory of arousal or activation which has been researched a great deal in the area of task performance and the variables which have been shown to affect it. Arousal level has been shown to correlate very strongly with certain bodily changes which can be monitored quite accurately and fairly easily. For instance, body temperature, electrical activity in the brain, heart rate, the ability of the skin to conduct electricity, are all liable to change in some way in response to the external environment. A full treatment of this concept of physiological arousal can be found in Grossman (1967). For many years it was considered that these changes were purely automatic and not in any way under the control of the organism. In fact these elements still go under the name of the autonomic nervous system, and to a very large extent the changes that occur in them do proceed without any conscious intervention from ourselves. The revolution came about with the discovery that these responses could be controlled to some extent by the organism itself at a conscious level providing the appropriate training was given. The research evidence also shows a firm relationship between the level of arousal and efficiency at carrying out tasks with a decrease in efficiency being observed when arousal proceeded beyond a certain level. The optimum level of arousal from the point of view of efficiency was shown to depend on the nature of the task. A further relationship was shown between the level of arousal and the subjective experience of calmness or anxiety. Schachter (1965) puts forward a theory which links arousal level with the cognitive labelling of emotions. Such a view accords with the position taken here regarding the neutrality of the 'tension . . . relaxation' continuum.


## MONITORING AROUSAL

There are two main methods which may be employed to monitor arousal level. The first may be described as an objective method where various instruments are used which give a visual or auditory signal. The second, and for the purposes of the techniques to be discussed in this book the most useful, is the more subjective method where the child himself learns to recognise the signals which are being passed to him by his body. A further possibility in the second method is the recognition of outwardly physical indications of arousal by the adult in charge of the child.

There is now available a whole range of small and readily portable instruments capable of providing direct information on the current state of the autonomic nervous system. It is possible to obtain a direct reading of heart rate, of skin temperature, of skin conductance — i.e. the ability of the skin to conduct electricity — of electrical activity in the muscles and of the electrical activity in the brain. It is usual for each response to be monitored by a separate instrument, but as there is a considerable degree of correlation between the different autonomic reponses this does not present any disadvantages. In fact this phenomenon presents quite distinct advantages in that it is possible to choose to use the instrument which is most convenient to set up, or is the lightest or, perhaps, the cheapest in the knowledge that the response being monitored is representative of the whole range of responses which could be monitored. Of course, for the purposes of research it is often vital to measure changes in a particular response or where the response to be monitored is itself the one to be controlled, e.g. heart rate or blood pressure. In these cases there is a need to employ a particular specialised instrument. Where, however, the need is only to acquire some indication of generalised arousal level, or more frequently, change of level, then the choice of instrument can be deter-mined by convenience.

There are two major ways in which information on the ongoing state of a particular response is presented. One method adopted is to provide a meter reading on some scale of high to low which is often quite accurately calibrated so that records may be kept of the readings. The other method is to provide a kind of auditory signal, usually in the form of clicks which can be set to commence at a predetermined level. The sound can act either as a warning signal to the child that he should carry out some previously learnt strategy or, as is more often the case, act as a signal confirming that he is successfully attaining his goal. For training purposes the authors have found this type of auditory feedback to be the most convenient and the most successful. Biofeedback techniques are frequently used by clinical psychologists in a variety of applications. Marcer (1986) provides a wide-ranging account of such applications and the instru-ments employed. In working with anxious children the authors have employed two major types of biofeedback instrument, one of which

35

depends on the fact that the skin excretes perspiration and the other which relies on the electrical activity which occurs within the muscles. These will now be described more fully.

## Skin conductance

The biofeedback instruments which monitor skin conductance rely on the fact that the sweat glands situated in the skin are very sensitive to changes in arousal level. It is possible to measure the resistance of the skin to the passage of small electric currents, and because the level of this resistance changes in line with the operation of the sweat glands it has been termed the galvanic skin response (GSR). For various technical reasons it has been found more useful to measure the ability of the skin to conduct rather than to resist the passage of electricity, and most biofeedback instruments which rely on the GSR now measure skin conductance.

In general, skin conductance increases with an increase in the level of arousal and decreases as the person becomes more relaxed. Slow changes in the level of conductance over periods of half an hour or so tend to indicate changes in the emotional state. Rapid changes may also be detected — with a delay as little as four seconds — following an attention-rousing event, e.g. a loud hand-clap. However, it is the former slow change in level which is important for monitoring movements on the 'tension . . . relaxation' continuum.

In order to monitor these changes or to give the person 'feedback' the instrument will typically provide visual presentation by means of a meter or an auditory presentation by means of a tone or clicks. This is achieved by placing two electrodes on the skin, usually on the finger-tips of the first and second fingers of one hand. Because the magnitude of the current passing is so tiny no sensation whatever is felt. The usual practice is to demonstrate the use of the instrument on one's own hand in order to alleviate any fears which may be aroused. No danger is involved as the instrument is powered by a low-voltage battery and there is no possibility of connection to the mains electricity.

Skin conductance biofeedback instruments vary according to the manufacturer, but we favour the type which can be adjusted to give feedback when the level of arousal decreases — i.e. as the child becomes more relaxed. The electrodes are connected to the fingers, and the instrument is adjusted so that no auditory feedback is present. The strategies that the child has learnt in order to bring about relaxation are then activated, and if they are successful the child will be 'rewarded' by the onset of the clicking sound. As he becomes more relaxed the frequency of the clicks increases over an interval of five seconds, at which time they cease and do not recur until he becomes yet more relaxed.

Some practitioners use these instruments for training in that all sessions would involve biofeedback, thus placing a great deal of reliance on externally provided information. Although in their early involvement with this type of therapy the authors adopted this approach, they now give much greater weight to the importance of internally experienced sensations of change in arousal level. The biofeedback instrument, when it is used at all, is employed as an occasional strategy to indicate to the child that the training he is undergoing is successful not only at the subjective level of feeling but also by referring to an objective measuring instrument.

**Figure 3.1:** A biofeedback instrument being used to monitor changes in skin conductance. The trainee receives the feedback either auditorily, by means of clicks, or visually, by way of the meter. Note the electrodes attached to the fingers.

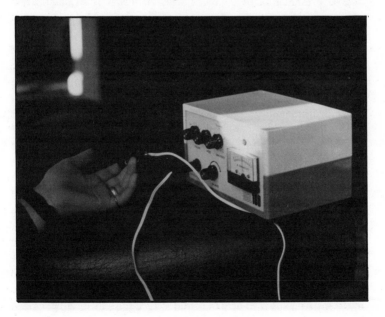

### The electromyograph

This is a more specialised instrument than the skin conductance apparatus described above. Its use is not advocated in the training of general relaxation techniques. However, it has been used extensively by the authors in their work with that special group of children who form the subject of Chapter 6, and for this reason some brief mention of the electromyograph (EMG) is appropriate here.

In order that any bodily movement can be made it is necessary for contractions to occur in the groups of muscles involved. These contractions are accompanied by electrical activity in the muscles, and the EMG is designed to measure these electrical potentials. Even when the body is held still a certain amount of firing will be taking place and this will only cease altogether when a muscle is completely relaxed. In order not to pre-empt the content of Chapter 6, suffice it to say that our aim with the group of children with whom we were working was to help them to voluntarily bring about a complete cessation of electrical activity in selected muscle groups.

The presentation of feedback with the EMG is similar to that described for the skin conductance instrument, i.e. visual by way of a meter and auditory by way of tone or clicks. Adhesive electrodes are placed on the surface of the skin just above the muscle group whose activity it is desired to monitor. The instrument is then set to provide auditory feedback when the electrical activity reaches a predetermined level. The child has to try to 'keep the muscle quiet'. The sensitivity of the instrument is progressively increased as the training strategies enable the child to attain greater control over the muscle firing. The next step for the child was to carry out a task using another group of muscles whilst still maintaining voluntary control over the muscles being monitored by the EMG.

These biofeedback instruments provide a useful external signal regarding the changes which are taking place internally, but they are by no means necessary to achieve the insights which training can bring. To some extent they may sometimes prove to be counterproductive if the child comes to rely too heavily on the external information, and by so doing fails to observe the signals which are available to him from paying attention to his own bodily feelings. The main use of the instruments is to help the child to recognise the bodily signals. It must be stressed that biofeedback instruments are not crucial to the acquisition of the techniques which will be dealt with later, and no recommendation is made that such instruments should be obtained for normal everyday use with children. They can of course, have

**Figure 3.2:** An electromyograph which is used to monitor electrical activity in groups of muscles. The instrument is shown in use in Chapter 6.

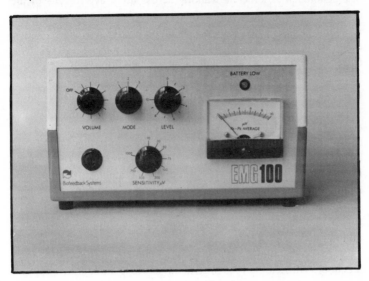

some value for therapists working regularly with numbers of different children, but they have only limited application in the home with parents working with their own children or in other situations where the children are well known to the adults in charge.

Much more important from the point of view of the approach adopted here is the ability to self-monitor arousal level. The message it is hoped to put across in this book is that the techniques of relaxation are available to everyone, and everyone may benefit from using them. Children are recognised to be in a much more vulnerable situation than adults with numerous messages being directed at them, some of them conflicting, some of these conflicting ones even coming from the same person or from different persons to all of whom he is expected to pay attention. Equipping children with the means to reduce their level of tension will ensure that they do not become overwhelmed with anxiety. Part of this training must be focused upon learning how to recognise the signs of increasing tension. These signs are readily available and well known both to adults and to children, although their significance is often missed.

There are levels of tension associated with particular experiences which are manifested in internal feelings so common that there exist expressions which seek to vividly describe them. For example, most people will understand precisely what is meant by having 'butterflies in the stomach', 'someone walking across my grave' or any of the other vividly descriptive expressions which give the essence of a sensation far more effectively than could more logical or scientific definitions. However, such descriptions tend to be concerned with the more extreme feelings, and although these are certainly very useful it is important to be able to recognise more subtle signals of increasing tension. There is also the problem posed by the fact that different people will experience the signs of tension in different ways. For this reason it is of crucial importance for parents and others who are close to children to be sensitive to the signals which are there to be seen by the observant. Both the authors have children, and some of the more subtle signs which have been observed amongst them include a paling of the face accompanied by an aura of withdrawal, walking on tiptoes and a rapid fluttering of the eyelids. Each of these was a sure sign of increasing tension in each of three children. It would be impossible to give a complete list of these more subtle signs for the very reason that they are peculiar to individual children. Fortunately it is not too difficult to recognise them, because the source of the tension is often known, and it is only necessary to be on the lookout for the signals with which the tension is accompanied.

In additon to subtle indications of increasing tension there are many signs shared by the majority of children. There is a very common tendency for children to show over-excited behaviour when tension is high, to show excessively dependent clinging behaviour or to complain of headache or stomach ache. Nail-biting, rocking, chattering, inappropriate laughter are other quite reliable indications of rising tension. However, a note of caution must be sounded here. You must know your child. Any of the signs mentioned could have significance when manifested by a child, but they may just as easily be without any significance at all as far as being indicants of tension goes. Once again, you must know your child.

## RELAXATION AND THE ENVIRONMENT

In the previous chapter a considerable amount was written regarding the effect of the environment on the development of tension. The same three aspects of the child's environment — the physical, the social and the personal — may be considered in relation to the other side of tension, or better, to the other end of the continuum — relaxation.

Much of the effect of the child's personal environment has been included in the discussion of the differing and subtle signs which children show of increasing tension. To some extent it would be possible to state that the absence of such signs would indicate a position closer to the relaxation end of the continuum. However, just as some of the signs of tension are subtle so are some of those which point towards relaxation. Steady breathing, a relaxed and comfortable body positon, arms and legs at rest and hands loose and still, are all readily available signs of relaxation to the observant adult. They can also come to be recognised by the child himself as messages about his own internal state.

The effect that the social environment has upon the 'tension . . . relaxation' continuum is usually much more under the control of parents, teachers and other adults than it is of the child. Clearly, the behaviour of the child will exert some influence over the social environment, but it is the responses and the initiatives taken by the adult which will have the most crucial effect. It is interesting to note how some children learn to provoke in adults the kind of responses which produce a tension-laden social environment. This apparently counterproductive behaviour usually has its roots in a quest for attention which the child has learnt cannot be gained by less irritating behaviour. Some consideration of the need to seek ways of positively controlling the social environment will be given in a later chapter. Suffice it to say here that a calm, quiet, good-humoured, non-reactive response to a child can bring a surprisingly rapid reduction of tension, to the greater benefit of all those present!

The physical environment may also be conceptualised as occupying a position on the continuum. Relaxation has been found to be more easily attained in a room or a setting where there is silence or only low-level noise, where there is little or no movement, where the visual environment is restful to the eyes and where the body is comfortable. These are all optimum conditions, and it is likely that relaxation in such surroundings will occur quite naturally. The trick is to bring it about when all the opposite conditions pertain!

## EMOTIONS AND LEARNING

The concept of tension and relaxation as occupying the opposite ends of a continuum which is emotionally neutral has been put forward, and will be returned to frequently in subsequent chapters. If this model is accepted then it is necessary to provide some explanation of the way in which different emotional states come to be related to different levels of 'tension . . . relaxation'. It is also necessary to deal with the apparent paradox of the same level of 'tension . . . relaxation' or arousal being associated with different emotional states. Both these phenomena can be dealt with satisfactorily by the proposition that emotions are learned behaviour.

Consider the previous section which dealt briefly with relaxation and the environment. Attention is drawn here to the possibility of conceptualising the environment itself, in its three different aspects of physical, social and personal, as occupying at any one time three different positions on the 'tension . . . relaxation' continuum. An example will help to explain the theory. Imagine a child, whose personal environment at a particular point in time is well towards the relaxation end of the continuum, entering upon a physical environment which is restful and quiet, to be greeted by a social environment where the adults are calm, good-humoured and reasonable. The child will experience an emotional state which is likely to be best described by words such as calm, placid, contented, secure. This internal emotional state will come to be associated with physical and social environments of the kind described, and the more often this occurs the stronger the association will become. It could well be that a particular room comes to be associated with a particular state even when the social environment is changed but, perhaps more importantly, the people or person in the social environment comes to be strongly associated with these emotions irrespective of the physical environment. This would explain why a child will remain calm and secure in the company of a particular adult even though there may be much in the physical environment which could be disturbing. Further, the same child may enter upon the same environment when his position on the 'tension . . . relaxation' continuum is towards the tension end, i.e. highly aroused. In this instance the previous association of the physical and social environments with a state of emotional calm will itself produce a learned response of calmness, and the level of arousal will be reduced.

The possibilities opened up by this approach to the development of a repertoire of emotional responses are virtually limitless. There are any number of levels of arousal that may be experienced in any number of physical environments in the presence of a potentially vast number of social environments. The interplay between these will bring about the learning of a huge number of emotional responses which could never be the same for two separate people however similar their experiences. It is because these vast possibilities exist for different emotional states becoming associated with different levels of arousal that the ability to learn techniques which can control the position on the 'tension . . . relaxation' continuum is so central to the message carried by this book. By giving to the child a means of reducing his level of arousal it is possible for him to activate learned emotional responses which may be more conducive to coping with a particular situation.

John is a pleasant and hard-working boy of good ability who is in the third year of his junior school. He is extremely popular with the other children and his teachers. He has the added advantage of being a competent sportsman. Unfortunately, he has one problem which has dogged him ever since he first entered school. He finds it quite impossible to cope with any class activity which could be interpreted as a test. His reaction to this is extreme — he flings himself out of the classroom and hotfoots it for home. If a teacher attempts to reason with him he is deaf to all logic, and if any attempt is made to physically restrain him he becomes quite violent. After such episodes he is always returned to school by his mother who is herself embarrassed whilst John is ashamed and contrite. Great concern is felt about how he will manage when he transfers to secondary education where tests of various kinds become a much more common ingredient of the educational feast. It is also recognised that whereas his problem is well known and managed sympathetically by the relatively small number of teachers who are responsible for him in the junior school, no such special treatment will be assured in the much more demanding environment of a large comprehensive school.

When interviewed by a psychologist, John is able to view his behaviour quite objectively and he expresses in fairly precise terms the internal feelings which he experiences immediately prior to his losing control. He is very highly motivated towards bringing about an end to these embarrassing incidents, and he enters enthusiastically upon a course of relaxation training. Within the space of three weeks he has learnt how to prevent these uncontrolled episodes from occurring. He is followed up for some years after he has transferred to his secondary school and not a single incident of the same nature is reported in spite of his finishing his school career by taking a number of public examinations.

This is a particularly useful illustrative example in that a number of

43

points may be drawn from it. Why John produced this extreme response when faced by the demand to take a test is not easy to explain. He did not need to fear obtaining a poor result because his work was good. Test results did not figure importantly in the assessment of the pupils. Children who did badly at them were never castigated in front of their classmates. The whole attitude towards tests was quite relaxed and non-threatening. Yet, somewhere in John's past experience he had learnt a fearful response towards them. Perhaps some chance juxtaposition of certain aspects of the physical, the personal and the social environments had combined to produce an innappropriate response which was so intense that learning took place immediately. No amount of logical and sympathetic reasoning could bring about a change in what could almost be described as an emotional flinch. Because this extreme response was so compelling for John no attempt to ensure that the physical and the social environment was non-threatening had any likelihood of producing an opposing learned response. His personal environment had to be altered by a self-activated technique designed specifically to reduce his tension level so that he felt relaxed and the extreme response was no longer appropriate.

## THE EXTREMES OF THE CONTINUUM

In the example given above John had produced a response to a tension-loaded situation which, on his own admission, was apparently beyond his control. He described himself as being taken over by a feeling which he could not control. Once under the influence of this over-powering emotion he produced a sequence of behaviour for which he did not seem to be responsible. He was quite sincere in his apologies after such an event, and he was being completely honest when he expressed the wish to his teachers and to his parents that he could stop acting in this way. To those who were able to observe John's behaviour at these times he appeared to be a completely different boy who was in the grip of an uncontrollable force.

The extremes of the continuum which have been discussed so far would not appear to allow for behaviour so much out of control as this. The tension end of the continuum has been characterised by emotions of anxiety and fear rather than the untrammelled emotion of panic which John was experiencing. Flight is a very common response to panic, and in some situations it is not innappropriate as, for instance, when fleeing from a danger which poses a bodily threat. Panic is a logical extension of the emotions related to the tension end of the continuum beyond those of anxiety and fear. What distinguishes it from the less extreme emotions is the extent to which it is disabling. In John's case this was self-evident. He was never going to be able to come to terms with the demands of a test situation if his only response was to run away. He would never be able to learn a new and more appropriate response to the situation because he was not around to do so. This was an extreme response to an extreme level of tension experienced by a child. However, it is suggested that the emotion of panic can be experienced with similarly disabling consequences which may not be visible at all to an outside observer.

Panic typically leads to a cessation of reasoned thought. It would seem that a more basic driving force than that of intellect takes over, with the consequence that the actions engaged in do not necessarily have a link with reality. As the behaviour produced is out of touch with reality then it is not amenable to reason, because at such a time reason is an aspect of that reality which is no longer available to the person. Also denied to a person who is experiencing a panic response is access to the pool of acquired knowledge which they have internalised. It is not unknown for students to write a whole set of answers to an examination paper consisting of unrelated nonsense, and yet to have no clear recollection of having done this. Panic can result in a response quite the opposite to the example given of running away. It can result in a freezing of activity where the person experiencing the emotion becomes incapable of thought or speech or any other voluntary physical action. Once again a variation in response is perceived as outward manifestations of internally felt emotion. Freezing, inappropriate actions and running away are vastly different responses but with one thing common to all of them. They are all disabling, and all lead to a complete loss of efficiency.

With such dangers attendant upon the increase of arousal beyond a certain level it is clearly important to devise ways of preventing this level from being reached. Firstly, the need to recognise the signs of increasing tension is paramount. This has already been touched upon, and more will be said later. Secondly, there must be available a technique which can be put into operation when the signs are recognised. Thirdly, the technique must be readily or even instantly available, and finally it must return the child to the relaxation end of the continuum or, at least, to that part of the tension range which does not lead to disabling emotions but to others which may facilitate the ability of the child to deal with the situation.

This is such an important sequence of events, crucial to the whole thrust of this book, that it is worthwhile to carefully consider the

45

**Figure 3.3:** Responses to a stressful situation

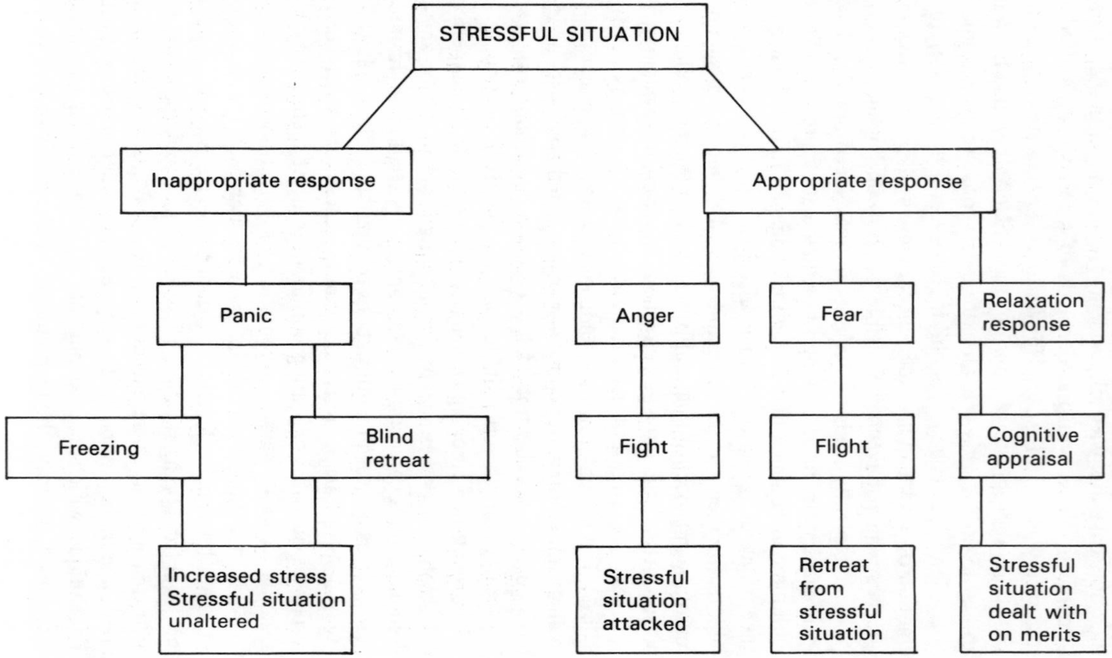

```
                          STRESSFUL SITUATION
                         /                    \
          Inappropriate response          Appropriate response
                 |                        /        |         \
               Panic                  Anger       Fear    Relaxation
              /     \                    |           |      response
          Blind   Freezing            Fight      Flight       |
         retreat                        |           |      Cognitive
            |       |               Stressful    Retreat    appraisal
        Increased stress            situation     from         |
        Stressful situation         attacked   stressful   Stressful
        unaltered                              situation   situation
                                                           dealt with
                                                           on merits
```

flow diagram shown in Figure 3.3.

So far the emphasis has been placed on the development of disabling emotional states related to the tension end of the continuum. Although much less obvious, and perhaps less often encountered, there are emotional states related to the relaxation end of the continuum which can also produce a decrease in performance. In certain situations it is possible to be too placid, contented and calm. An athlete preparing for an important event does not benefit by being so relaxed that he makes no emotional investment in his performance. A child confronted with examinations who is so calm that the thought of doing well or doing badly does not enter into his consideration at all is unlikely to achieve particularly good results.

Anthony is a very bright boy of 16 who is due to take public examinations at his secondary school. He is considered a charming lad by all those who know him, but he is driving his teachers and his parents to distraction because of his apparently uncaring attitude towards the impending examinations. This is not because he is rejecting the compulsion to study hard — he does this. It is not because he does not appreciate the need to do well in the examinations — he dearly wants to go to university. For some reason he just cannot be persuaded to put more than the minimum effort into the papers. When he is seen by a psychologist the unusual conclusion is reached that here is a boy who is insufficiently aroused. The emotions he experiences when he writes his answers are those associated with the relaxation end of the continuum. He feels perfectly at ease, calm, placid, unconcerned. This under-aroused state is incompatible with the motivation to do well, and accounts for his relatively unsatisfactory performance. It is decided that a direct method should be adopted to increase his level of arousal and a programme is devised which involves Anthony in short bursts of hard physical exercise immediately prior to his undertaking the exams. He is given physical targets which he has to work to exceed so that not only is he more highly aroused physically but there is a mental element involved as well. Much to the surprise of his somewhat sceptical parents and teachers the strategy produces the desired effect. The psychologist is highly gratified with the validation of his hypothesis, and perhaps a little surprised, too!

This example provides a possible explanation of those children who are so often described as idle, uninterested or unmotivated by their teachers. This is an especially persuasive idea when these same children may be observed working for long periods on tasks which interest them, i.e. tasks which for the child has an intrinsic ability to raise the level of arousal, or can be seen excelling at sport — another type of activity with an intrinsically arousing component. Certainly, the suggestion fits comfortably into the theory of the 'tension . . . relaxation' continuum and will merit further investigation.

# 4

# Tension Management

*The case has been made that anxiety is related to a level of arousal that is so high as to be disabling. As well as the further development of the concept of over-arousal, this chapter also examines the more novel notion of under-arousal.*

The previous chapter dealt with relaxation as being the other side of tension, and concluded with an example of a boy whose problem lay in his low level of arousal. Even in a potentially anxiety-provoking situation the point on the 'tension . . . relaxation' continuum at which he operated was such that his emotional involvement was characterised by placidity, calmness and detachment. This type of problem is almost certainly much more widespread than would be imagined from the frequency with which parents and teachers seek help with its alleviation. This is quite understandable in that such behaviour rarely gives rise to the intensity of concern given by those states associated with high levels of tension. A child who is observed as having a very calm and placid outlook on life is not usually rated as being in need of help, although his teachers and his parents may suggest that a charge of dynamite placed in near proximity to him might serve to wake him up!

From the point of view of the child himself the situation is also quite different from that which assails the child who operates nearer to the tension end of the continuum. The next chapter concludes with an account of Joanne who developed anorexia. For some time she used this to take control of her situation which included assuming control over others. It was not until her weight loss had proceeded to a point where she collapsed and had to be rushed to hospital that anxiety developed. From this time she was able, at last, to make a realistic assessment of her situation and become amenable to therapy.

Children such as Anthony and Joanne present widely differing problems, yet both may have their origins in the inappropriateness of the degree of tension or relaxation experienced. In Joanne's case, or in others where anxiety is experienced, the child may well be uneasy or unhappy, and will respond to help enthusiastically because he perceives himself as someone who has a problem. For example, he knows that he loses his temper too easily or that he 'freezes' when he becomes anxious. He shares similar worries about his behaviour with the adults around him. Contrast this with a child such as Anthony whose arousal level is too low — he is unconcerned about his emotional state because it is a very comfortable one. Indeed, it is just such a state that many of the children who are the subjects of this book would aspire to, or which would be sought on their behalf by their parents.

It is curious that the efforts which have so far been made to utilise the findings associated with arousal theory have tended to be concentrated in two quite separate and independent areas. These are the areas typified by the two extremes of the continuum. On the one hand some work has been carried out with anxiety-ridden people or those who are going to be faced with potentially anxiety-provoking situations. On the other hand there has been a considerable amount of research directed at discovering the optimum conditions under which people engaged in monotonous but vital tasks will maintain their concentration. Much of this research is reviewed in Davies and Tune (1970). A number of examples have already been given of children who have experienced emotions typical of the tension end of the continuum, but these are not so easy to find with regard to the relaxation end because the emphasis has not been on people experiencing difficulties but rather on people engaged in tasks. Some illustrations of this approach will help to provide the framework into which will be set the concept of low-level arousal and the steps that can be taken to deal with it.

During the Second World War the development of new technology, particularly in the field of radar, required military personnel to sit for long periods in front of a display watching for a signal. This signal might well consist of a small and ill-defined smudge of light appearing on a screen for a brief period amongst a number of other similar signals. A typical example of this would be in a convoy of merchant ships where the escorting vessels would see on their radar screens the 'blips' representing the ships in their care and would need to be alert for any additional 'blips' that could not be accounted for. In order to concentrate the attention of the operator the radar would normally be sited in a darkened room where distraction could be kept to a minimum. Unfortunately, such conditions and such a monotonous task tend to lead to a decrease in attention, drowsiness and even sleep. Not surprisingly, a great deal of effort was soon being directed into determining the best conditions under which such vigilance tasks could be undertaken. A whole new field of psychological research opened up which examined the effects of a wide range of factors which impinged upon this vital task of maintaining alertness in what were essentially boring situations. These included such things as the length of time operators spent on the task, the time of day, the quality of the signal, the frequency of missing a signal compared with the false identification of a non-existent signal. Attention was given to the environment in which the task took place, the effect of 'clutter' on the screen and the degree of urgency perceived in the task. It was not long before the individual differences between different operators were taken into account and means were sought of identifying people who would excel at such a task. One of the methods by which it was thought that this could be achieved was to look at basal levels of arousal as indicated by various physiological measures such as heart rate, skin conductance, EEG patterns, etc. That this method proved to be unsuccessful should not come as a surprise to readers of this book, who will already be aware of the complexity of the factors which determine the point occupied on the 'tension . . . relaxation' continuum at any given moment in time. However, in common with a great deal of research activity that does not achieve its intended goal, the 'spin-off' in terms of other useful knowledge gained was quite considerable. For example, it became clear that at least two identifiable groups of people exist where the basal level of arousal differed. Because so many other factors were involved this did not lead to any particularly useful means of selecting good radar operators, but it does fit in well with the approach adopted here where individual differences in emotional response are related to some innate level of tension as well as to all the other environmental factors. To what extent these innate differences come about as a result of genetic inheritance, and how much the difference is due to exposure to unique environmental experience, is problematical. A good discussion of the role played by individual differences in vigilance tasks can be found in Burch and Kanter (1984).

The concept of tension management should be considered not only in relation to the ability to deal with individual situations as they arise, or even as a means to maintain a comfortable position on the continuum, although the achievement of both of these aims would be beneficial. A third, and perhaps more important, aspect of tension management is the manner in which a child comes to have a particular basal level of arousal. Clearly, the level of arousal experienced by different people will vary greatly even when they are 'at rest'. Some people will be very relaxed and apparently at ease with themselves, whilst others will always seem to be slightly on edge or alert. These are outward signs of basal arousal level.

It must be accepted that an unknown proportion of this basal level of arousal is due to an innate genetic predisposition, and it is probably wise to accept that nothing can be done about changing this. However, that still leaves an also unknown proportion of this basal level as being accounted for in terms of environmental experience. Anxious and worried parents tend to have children who demonstrate similar characteristics. Placid and calm parents frequently have contented children. If, however, it is possible to change an individual's position on the continuum by teaching relaxation then this should have some implications for parenthood. To put this differently, parents who recognise themselves as being anxious, worried or quick to lose their tempers can best help their children by doing something about themselves. Such parents would be well advised to carry out the relaxation training outlined in Chapter 1.

A great deal of children's learning comes about as a consequence of imitation, which then becomes so deeply internalised that it ceases to be imitation and forms part of the child's response pattern. It is, of course, an important part of the message carried here that this response pattern can be changed, but it is worthwhile to remember that a significant part of this pattern is determined by the adults within the child's environment and for these adults to endeavour to act accordingly.


## LOW-LEVEL TENSION MANAGEMENT

Although the problems associated with a basal arousal level which is located towards the lower extreme of the 'tension . . . relaxation' continuum tend to be of a kind which are not recognised as being a cause for serious concern it could be argued that these may be just as disabling for the child as those problems which are clearly there for everyone to see. Many children go through their entire school career with the reputation of being lazy, unmotivated, uncaring and workshy. It is only necessary to think of the thousands of the 'could do better' category of remarks, under which so many of our children's school reports lie submerged, to become aware of the ubiquity of these problems. Not all the failure to come up to the expectations of teachers and of parents could be ascribed to a low level of arousal — without doubt some children remain uninterested in school work for the very simple reason that so often school work is uninteresting. It is often seen only as a means to an end, and providing the end is recognised as being sufficiently valuable some children will work hard to achieve it. Others will not feel the same motivation, and for some of these, perhaps for many of these, the cause will be located in too low a level of arousal.

If a low basal level of arousal is accepted as a reason for the poor school performances achieved by large numbers of children then two dilemmas immediately become apparent. The first of these is concerned with how this may be recognised and the second is concerned with the steps that may be taken to alleviate it. In dealing with the problem of identification it is necessary for teachers and parents to bear in mind that there are at least two possibilities which exist here. Some children are unmotivated because there is little in the teaching and the curriculum content to excite them. In this case it is for the teachers to accept that looking for the fault within the child is a barren exercise and to show a willingness to attend instead to their own short-comings. The second possibility, i.e. that the problem lies within the child whose basal arousal level is too low, is one that may be approached from a number of angles.

The first requirement is for the adult to look objectively at the environment. This is by no means an easy task as the adult is usually a central part of it and may, to a large extent, be responsible for its nature. In school a teacher should consider the attitude of the other children in the group. It if can be honestly stated that the majority of the children seem to enjoy their work, come into the classroom enthusiastically and do not seek excuses to be doing something else then it would be reasonable to look for the cause within the child. Are there some lessons in which the child plays a full part, or is the same lack of motivation demonstrated in all lessons? Does he enter into some activities outside school with a commitment and enthusiasm never seen in the classroom? A similar set of observations can be made by parents, and a similar set of questions asked about the child's behaviour in the home. If such an objective searching of the environment results in a sincere and genuine conviction that the fault does not lie there then it may be reasonable to consider the possibility that there is a problem connected with low arousal.

Some of the signs of low-level arousal are fairly easy to recognise once the adult has become sensitive to them. Most people are somewhat sluggish at the beginning of the day but does this persist well into the morning? Does it only disappear when some exciting activity is imminent? Does the child seem to be more alert and respon-sive immediately after some strenuous physical activity? Does he take a long time to get started on a task? Does he sometimes surprise his teachers or his parents with a burst of energy? Does he sometimes produce a piece of work vastly superior to his customary efforts? If the answer to some of these questions is positive then it would appear to be worthwhile to consider what can be done about increasing the level of arousal.

It would be dishonest to suggest that the strategies available for assisting children to attain a point nearer the tension end of the 'tension . . . relaxation' continuum are anywhere near as well developed as those concerned with bringing about a reduction of this level. For the authors this is a relatively new and exciting field into which they have entered. Many puzzling questions regarding children's behaviour which have confronted them in the past seem to become amenable to being answered when looked at in the light of this new approach. Some strategies have already been developed and are being rewarded with success, and it would seem appropriate even at this early stage to recommend them to parents, teachers and other adults as being worthy of a trial. The approaches adopted so far may be subdivided into direct and indirect methods.

## DIRECT APPROACHES

When dealing with the more customary problems associated with too high a level of tension the child is helped to recognise the internally experienced signs of tension build-up. He is taught strategies which may be used at such times to lower this level so that he is then able to deal with the tension-provoking activity or situation with a more relaxed approach. In the case of a child who fails to achieve his potential because of too low a level of arousal the first task would be to help him to recognise that this does exist as a problem for him. The type of signals available to the over-aroused child would seem to be missing in this case. However, this may not necessarily be true. It may only be that the signals are not so universally recognisable as those associated with fear, anger or apprehension. They are likely to be more easily recognised by the other members of the child's social environment than by the child himself. An unwillingness to start an activity irrespective of whether it is work or play, an easy acceptance by the child of levels of achievement well below his potential, an emotional 'flatness' — these are some of the signs which might be observed.

The usual response of adults to such signs is to attempt to reason with the child about his lack-lustre approach or, perhaps more commonly, to try to bully him out of it. Most adults who have faced such problems would have to agree that both approaches have met with little success. Even though the child may be stung into some activity it is likely that it will still be characterised by unwillingness or sluggishness. This may be explained by the low arousal level with which the activity is accompanied. The key to the problem is to bring about an increase in this level, preferably by the application of learnt techniques by the child himself. This is a direct approach to low-level tension management and it involves a form of training which is aimed at increasing the level of the autonomic responses, i.e. precisely the opposite to that form of training adopted for the anxious child. Because these autonomic responses can be placed under the control of the child — and this can quite definitely be achieved with appropriate training — there is no logical reason why the voluntary intervention should not be aimed at achieving an increase in arousal level instead of the more usual decrease. There exists good laboratory evidence for the attainment of increased levels of arousal although the techniques used have invariably relied on the use of biofeedback instruments. As psychologists the authors have used methods involving these instruments with under-aroused children, but we do not now believe such external aids to be necessary. Some training techniques which might be explored are dealt with in a later chapter.

## INDIRECT APPROACHES

It is not at all unusual when carrying out research into some apparently new form of therapy, whether the concern is physiological or psychological, to discover that others in a different guise have passed that way before. The action of new drugs has frequently been predated by herbalist remedies. The whole field of alternative medicine is now having to be taken seriously and it is acknowledged that many of the practices originated far back in the past. Likewise, in seeking indirect methods for bringing about an increase in arousal level the evidence is clear that such methods already exist, although their rationale is expressed differently. Some older readers will no doubt recall that it was not at all unusual for the school day to begin with a session of 'physical jerks' standing behind the desks in the classroom. These required mental concentration as they had to be carried out in unison, and physical application as they had to be carried out energetically. Not a bad way of increasing arousal level! What effect they had upon the already anxious child can only be a matter for speculation! It would not be at all surprising if many of the incorrect answers, blurted out in the table tests which invariably followed such drill, were a consequence of over-anxiety rather than under-learning.

Such practices are quite normal in Japan where the working day in many of their factories commences with a session of communal physical training. From the successes achieved by Japanese industry it would seem that raising the arousal level of the workers must be a contributory factor. If production levels are to be considered the hallmark of success then such procedures would seem to be wholly laudable, but the crucial element which is unaccounted for in such a regime is the existence of individual differences. There is no case to be made for increasing the arousal level of someone already motivated to commence work, and there may well be actual harm done by increasing the arousal level of those who are already apprehensive and anxious. The consequences of such procedures may not be observed on the production line but personal lives may be less happily affected.

In the case of children, where the insight into their own problem is lacking because of immaturity or low intellect, some kind of indirect approach based upon physical activity might be usefully adopted. It should only be used where there is very good reason to believe that the cause of the problem is a too low position on the 'tension . . . relaxation' continuum bearing in mind the cautions outlined earlier in this chapter. There should also be no hint of such techniques being used as a punishment for not trying hard enough or for being lazy.

Much preferred amongst the indirect methods which may be adopted are those where the child is taught the techniques to bring about an increase in the level of arousal in much the same way as where a direct method is to be employed. In the case of relaxation training where the appropriate use of the technique is beyond the ability of the child to comprehend, methods will be suggested whereby the adult can provide a cue for the child as a means of preparing him for the test or enabling him to cope with the potentially anxiety-provoking situation. Similar methods will be discussed for the under-aroused child where the adult can trigger the already learnt arousing techniques.

## HIGH-LEVEL TENSION MANAGEMENT

The current level at which a child is operating on the 'tension . . . relaxation' continuum will depend upon a variety of factors. Many of these have already been discussed, and in Chapter 7 an attempt will be made to draw them all together into a systematised framework.

The crucial point which is intended to come out of this approach is that the ability to carry out any activity efficiently will depend upon the current level of tension being appropriate for that activity. Most people will recognise that it is possible to experience a mismatch between their current emotional state and the demands of the situation in which they are placed. Consider, for example, a child who sets out for school having witnessed a violent argument between his parents concerning whether or not he should be punished for some mis-demeanour. Unless this is such a common occurrence in his life that he has become habituated to it, he will almost certainly experience a whole range of conflicting emotions. Without examining in any detail the nature of these emotions it can be assumed that his position on the 'tension . . . relaxation' continuum is most likely to be towards the tension end. Upon arriving at school he may be required to put his mind to a task which calls for calm and logical thought and the need to concentrate. There will, however, inevitably exist a mismatch between the optimum level of tension required for the task and the level of tension being experienced by the child. The likely result of this mismatch will be a failure on the part of the child to achieve the success of which he is capable. The outward signs of this inappropriate tension level might be a lack of concentration manifested by day-dreaming, inaccuracies in written work or, with some children, overt attention-seeking behaviour.

A fairly dramatic example has been given above in order to illu-strate the point as vividly as possible, but much less obvious situations may produce inappropriate tension levels. The task itself may be associated with previously experienced failure. This failure may have been dealt with unsympathetically: it may have led to derision or even to contempt. The emotions felt at such treatment would have been linked to a level of tension which, in turn, would be experienced again on being confronted with a similar task or with the same teacher. It can readily be seen how a vicious circle of failure can be established which does not, in fact, necessarily rest upon the child's inability to learn the task, but only upon his inability to learn it when in a disabling state of tension.

Although school occupies a very important aspect of the life of a child, and it is there that the most obvious consequences of the extremes of 'tension . . . relaxation' continuum may be most readily observed, it should not be thought that the school has the monopoly of such consequences. Children at home will also manifest the behavioural and emotional states which can come about because of a level of tension that is too high. Consider the common example of the child who behaves in an over-excited way when callers come to the home. Many parents will know the extremes of embarrassment felt when their normally sensible child acts like a spoilt brat in front of visitors. For a child, the appearance of a guest in the home is an exciting event, with a consequent increase in the level of tension. The emotional states associated with this higher level of tension could include anxiety, fear, anger, volatility, aggressiveness, to name only a few. None of these are particularly appropriate to the business of entertaining a guest! Unfortunately, the customary responses to behaviour related to these emotions is calculated to bring about a further increase in the level of tension rather than causing its reduction. These responses tend to reflect the anger, embarrassment and irritation felt by the parents and the final consequences are usually disastrous for all concerned. A recognition of what is happening to the child to produce the unwanted behaviour could lead to the positive use of tension management techniques.

It would be quite wrong to assume that all the emotions associated with the higher levels of tension are of necessity disabling. Reference has already been made to the need for an athlete to experience some degree of anticipation prior to an event and, for some athletes, this could even be a feeling of apprehension. It must always be borne in mind that individual differences in basal levels of arousal will affect the individually experienced level of tension which is the optimum for any one person in any one situation. Part of the training in tension management must be directed towards recognising this optimum level.

Many motorists will be aware that too high a level of tension brings about a worsening of their driving skills. This often arises as a consequence of impatience, intolerance of other road users or any of the other irritating conditions met with on the road. They will also be aware that the tensional level brought about by domestic or business conflict may also change the character of their driving. Less appreciated is the reduction in driving skills which comes about as a consequence of monotony, under-stimulation, sleep-deprivation and other factors which bring about a disabling level of relaxation. This example, although not specifically pertinent to children, does serve to point up the concept of an optimum level of arousal for the efficient discharge of a task. This is most easily appreciated in those tasks where physical activity predominates, such as various forms of sport, driving and manual work. Not so readily seen, but still evident to the sensitive observer, is the effect upon speech, writing and various creative skills. Such losses in efficiency are very closely related to the well-known consequences of fatigue. When tired it is difficult to marshal thoughts logically. When tired it is difficult to generate creative ideas. When tired it is easy to make undetected mistakes. Similar problems may occur when under-aroused for reasons other than fatigue — for instance, low basal arousal level, low motivation or lack of stimulation. In all such cases the optimum level of arousal is absent.

## CHRONIC DISABLING TENSION

There exists the possibility of tension increasing to a point where it becomes disabling. The next chapter gives an example of this and refers to such an eventuality as the 'panic response'. This is an extreme response which for most people will occur only rarely; for some not at all. There is, however, one group of people whose normal state bears some resemblance to this extreme position on the 'tension . . . relaxation' continuum. It is the physical rather than the emotional nature of the disablement which is typified by this group in that the limbs fail to carry out the messages transmitted by the brain, or only succeed in carrying them out imperfectly. In a subsequent chapter the lessons learnt by working with some children from this group are used to illuminate and inform the work carried out with 'normal' children.

# 5

## De-fusing Anxiety

*Anxiety can be explosive in the sense that it is associated with chaos and loss of direction and control. Therefore it has to be de-fused — a cool, calm constructive approach is needed.*

The range of behaviour, between being anxious and being relaxed, has been described as belonging to a continuum. This is the 'tension . . . relaxation' continuum which can be thought of as relatively neutral. We may examine this concept further.

In our everyday experience we have feelings, and these we can express in physiological terms. When highly aroused, for instance, we may become aware of certain reactions within ourselves — amongst which there is a quickening of the pulse, the heart beats faster, breathing and perspiration become noticeably different. If, on the other hand, what is experienced at any given time is a feeling of calm and inner peace, the body is relatively inert. Pulse, heart rate, breathing are as normal, and the sweat glands function in line with the ordinary demands of the body. The analogy with the anxious state is not accidental. A person aroused to a pitch of anxiety is also physiologically aroused to a higher level. Anxiety is characterised by the 'high' physiological state described above: in short the body gets set to avoid whatever is producing that anxiety.

Evolution necessitates that this is so. Without an avoidance mechanism man would not have survived the variety of threatening situations in his environment. But what further characterises anxiety is that it is an unnecessary response to environmental hazards. For we often respond anxiously to what we perceive as threatening situations, even when logically they offer no real danger at all. Consider the panic response.

Someone is sitting at his desk on the third floor of the office building. A door opens and a faint whiff of smoke permeates the air. Instantly distracted, our office worker steps briskly to the door. The smell is stronger now. He is convinced the building is on fire and he must leave it as soon as possible. Perfectly reasonably too, you might say. A moment's thought, however, and he might have paused to wonder why no-one else seems too concerned. Communication with downstairs is on-going and the third floor occupants know of the workmen who are stripping the paintwork on the second floor. Our friend knows too, but his heart tells him of hidden dangers. It is fairly racing and his stomach is in knots as he takes his seat again. He cannot concentrate on his papers when his fingers fumble and a clammy sensation chills his soul. The carefree attitude of his colleagues serves only to heighten his fears: all they ever think about is clearing their desks and meeting management targets; then it's talk and activity geared to what they are going to do after work. But they'll never see the realisation of today's efforts, there'll be no leisure time to enjoy — we'll all be fried alive in this awful building! Wide-eyed, he finds himself staring at the Emergency exit. To hell with them, he must get out!

Panic has taken over. He charges through the room, down the stairs, knocking others out of his way, creating mayhem as he flees terror-stricken from the building. There is no fire; nor are there any reasonable grounds for supposing there is. His reaction is quite irrational, an expression of his phobia of fires. Any initial concern he might have had was superseded at pace by pre-eminent anxiety; his phobic reaction ensured that this anxiety spiralled. Furthermore, if the same situation arose again his reaction is likely to be just as alarmist, because physiologically this is how he is set to react, and his panic response is continually being reinforced by the fact that he always takes action to avoid the danger he perceives. No matter there was no danger in the first place, he has made sure of safety anyway. What he has not done is take control of the associated anxiety. Had he done so, and were he to do so again, his handling of dangerous situations would be much more rational. For associated with being in control as opposed to being anxious are a steady heart beat, a regular pulse, relaxed breathing, hands, brain and body all geared to operating with maximum efficiency.

Just as it is possible to learn to react anxiously to certain situations, so is it possible to learn a different pattern of response. The alternative response is necessary to break the anxiety spiral. What prompts an effective alternative response is the actual tension the body experiences in the face of the anxiety-provoking situation. The latter can become the cue for its own reduction! For the person who reacts to unwanted and unnecessary tension by using a relaxation strategy to manage it is acting to prevent its escalation into crippling anxiety.

To be able to adopt a more positive strategy demands a more

61

objective appraisal of the situation. Initially one may have to rely on a therapist or some other third party to formulate such a rational strategy to deal with possible anxiety-provoking situations. However, that is not always necessary. What is needed in the longer term is that one will have sufficient grasp of a relaxation technique which can be applied whenever needed. This can certainly be learned, and at least as well by children as by adults.

## OBSERVATION OF BEHAVIOUR: A MORE OBJECTIVE APPROACH

Perception of behaviour in terms of the continuum 'tension . . . relaxation' is one way of playing down the more usual emotive connotations of that behaviour. It allows the more objective appraisal of the child's behaviour, which is necessary if the child is to learn an alternative response. Whether the appraisal is by the adult *in loco parentis*, by the child or by both, it has to be rid as far as possible of any obstructive connotations, any heavy emotive overlay, any clutter or side-tracking vibrations.

The sort of language we regularly use to describe behaviour, and particularly behaviour we dislike, is often prejudicial to any reasonable, objective assessment. And when it comes to describing children's behaviour, especially if we find it upsetting in any way . . . the adjectives commonly used to depict the child and what he is up to, usually over-state the case, saying more about our feelings as the caring adult than about the actual behaviour we witness in the child. Moreover, we tend to use our vocabulary to describe the child rather than what he is doing. But perceiving someone as tense or relaxed has patent physiological implications, as distinct from using descriptions which have obvious or latent social or moral bias. If the attention of the caring adult can be directed towards observing the child's behaviour, and if sharper observation techniques can be developed, then the observer becomes quite subtly involved in interpreting the behaviour sensitively, rather than commenting, usually adversely, on the child himself. It is important to recognise what is being described, the child or the behaviour. Arguably, it is impossible to assess objectively in any meaningful way the child as a person, especially when the adult has care of that child as parent, teacher, social worker, etc. When you are 'involved' how objective can you be? But some measure of objectivity in observing actual behaviour is certainly possible, and often both the observations and the incidence of the behaviour are quantifiable and even measurable. When relative degrees of tension or relaxation are what we perceive, then we have a sound basis for an objective form of assessment.

It might be instructive to examine at this point a number of adjectives and descriptive terms commonly used in the context of children and how they behave. It is difficult to find any terminology to express adult concerns about children which does not carry pejorative connotations.

---

Below is a list of adjectives and expressions frequently used to describe children and/or their behaviour. Rate these descriptive terms 1 to 7, to correspond with the scale of this 'tense . . . relaxed' continuum. Take a sheet of paper, copy the headings and scale given below, and write in each of these terms according to your own interpretation of what they mean.

<----very   tense--tense--<< >>--relaxed--very   relaxed-->
1........2.........3.........4.........5.........6........7

| | | |
|---|---|---|
| rough | studious | attention-seeking |
| wild | boisterous | gentle |
| reasonable | impetuous | calm |
| quiet | rowdy | peaceable |
| noisy | headstrong | soft |
| disorderly | excitable | placid |
| sedate | sensible | good-natured |
| highly strung | overpowering | easy-going |
| meek | tolerant | uncontrollable |
| restless | unruffled | erratic |
| impulsive | easily led | impatient |
| composed | hot-headed | fretful |
| hasty | indolent | aggressive |
| touchy | nervous | considerate |
| maladjusted | withdrawn | weak |
| spineless | lively | fidgety |
| ill-at-ease | hyperactive | dreamy |
| disturbed | self-assured | dull |
| eager | sleepy | spirited |
| dopy | irritating | comfortable |
| demanding | slow | clumsy |

You are probably finding that columns 2 and 3 ('very tense'

---

and 'tense' on our scale) and also columns 5 and 6 ('relaxed' and 'very relaxed') are collecting most of your descriptive words. Why? Because these words are readily associated by you with each other, with what you regard as socially or morally acceptable as well as with the headings given. But the headings are more neutral than the terms you have organised into the columns, in the sense that they have direct physiological connotations which of themselves do not necessarily conjure up ideas of acceptance or rejection.

It is alarmingly easy, however, to use an emotive term (e.g. 'headstrong' or 'easily led') rather than a more neutral form of words. If instead you are in a position to observe that there is a tautening of the muscles — the forehead puckers, for instance — then your observation can be made without any overtones or bias implicit or explicit in what you say, think, or in how you react. The trick is to observe what you see in as detached (neutral) a manner as possible.

It will be readily appreciated that many of the terms above are decidedly less neutral than the headings, 'tense' and 'relaxed'. The latter, it is argued, are a more helpful interpretation because they lead to more constructive action. They refer, perhaps only implicitly, to the physiological state. Colloquially, they take the steam out of the situation and prepare the ground for the essential task of 'de-fusing' any anxiety either incipient or actual.

One of the greatest difficulties for us as parents is to learn to stand back and take a dispassionate view of the difficulties facing the child. Such distancing of self from child is viable and essential in the interests of observing, noting and assessing the actual behaviour of the child. Some measure of detachment is always helpful in this assessing process. It is worth distinguishing, however, between assessing and teaching. Since good teaching includes providing support, guidance and reinforcement, it has to be the whole parenting self that is made available to the child. But in both activities the caring parent is assisting in developing a strategy whereby the child's problem can be tackled constructively. The parent is helping to de-fuse the potentially explosive situation of anxiety.

The distinction between assessing and teaching, however, becomes blurred, in so far as both processes become integrated within the working relationship which exists between, say, parent and child — a point registered in Hersen and Bellack's (1976) introduction to the whole subject of behavioural assessment. What in effect happens is that as soon as the parent or acting parent learns to 'stand back' from the child and his anxieties, there is an immediate boost to the child's learning a strategy to cope; the parent has created the enabling conditions for the child to learn.

Acquisition of the skills to take a long, hard look at one's behaviour — what may have caused it, the actual behaviour itself and its effects on self or others — is a growth point for any child. Useful learning can now follow. For it is the prelude to developing a means of changing some form of behaviour or reacting that is unproductive or inefficient, perhaps anti-social or even amoral. Such reactions are often considered deviant in the sense that they tend to be unacceptable and so become associated, directly or indirectly, with anxiety for the child.

For the parent who knows her child it is not too difficult to judge whether the child is relaxed or tense. There are recognisable signs, including physical and physiological expressions, which correlate with these states. Loss of appetite, disturbed sleep, a moody or despairing presence around the house, nervous mannerisms, restlessness, reports of deterioration in performance from school or elsewhere, or increased demands for attention are some of the indicators. Parents must watch out for them. Mum and dad together can sit down in a moment of calm and pin-point the factors relevant to a state of excessive tension in their own child. It is only when anxiety is recognised that appropriate action to do something about it can then be taken.

It is again worth emphasising that parents who identify behaviour in terms of the 'tension . . . relaxation' continuum do so without great risk of social or moral stigma for their child. If parents hear others speak of their child as neurotic or wild or hyperactive, as disturbed or moody or withdrawn, then their own anxiety is likely to be exacerbated. The relationships mum and dad have with their child, already under siege, will be aggravated further. While they may feel powerless to influence the perceptions of others, it is certainly worth considering to what extent they may help matters by adopting a more helpful attitude themselves by defining their own child's behaviour in their own terms. Accordingly, perception in terms of the 'tension . . . relaxation' continuum is more palatable to the parent and to others, as well as more useful to the child. It doesn't hurt as much, and encourages one to think of solutions. These are solutions, too, which are very much within the management and control of child and parents. Relaxation training and its appropriate application offers far more than the helplessness which often drives parents to seek explanatory diagnostic labels, such as: your child is 'maladjusted', 'delinquent', etc.

These are the sort of labels associated with professional agencies. Yet in recent years the whole business of labelling children at all has come under fierce attack, not only from parents but from the professionals themselves. Labelling is clearly a matter of who sees what. One man's 'maladjusted' is another's 'lively'; for the phrase 'could do better', read 'I don't know how to teach him'. Whereas the doting parent may describe her son as 'sensitive', the beleaguered teacher of a group of disillusioned fourth-formers may be driven to depict the lad as 'a pain in the neck'. This is a common situation and readily recognised. The use of labels to categorise behaviour is usually not very helpful. Moreover, in the context of discussion about the so-called behaviour disorders, one effect of labelling and so identifying a child with other children with known behavioural disorders and with other behaviours just as intractable is to increase the anxiety felt about that child and his difficult behaviour. Professionals tend to persist in the use of labels in order to communicate in shorthand to other professionals just what sort of behaviour they are talking about when describing children. However, one effect of recent legislation has been to bring parents and professionals closer together in examining their joint responsibilities towards the education of the children under their care, and so both are encouraged to employ the same terminology when describing their charges.

The professional agencies tend to assume that their approach to the child is more reasoned, more objective. It can be, but need not be. It is generally accepted that the professional contact lacks the emotional bond of the parent/child relationship and so the professional is more detached than mum or dad. Parents love, and regrettably do occasionally hate, their offspring — for all sorts of reasons, not least because they often see in their child something of themselves. But they are almost never indifferent to their own flesh and blood. The parent/child relationship is intense, whereas contact between the employed professional and the client child has to be, and is, more detached, a step or two removed from direct responsibility for the actions of that child.

Whilst all of the above may be obvious, yet the perception of the professional person is also amenable to distortion. The professional is first and foremost a person, and usually a very committed person at that, whose chosen field of endeavour is to work for children. All of us, parents and professionals, must view people and situations from the standpoint of what we are and our experience of life. The professional's perception of events is going to be less influenced by wholly subjective considerations than that of a child's parents, but is nonetheless subject to the effects of one's training and experience, the intensity of involvement with the client, one's perception of what is and is not acceptable, and is in any case coloured by values of which the child may have had little or no experience.

So the task for the professional in seeking objectivity of appraisal resembles that of the parent or any other interested party: we all have to stand back and record, if possible measure, the behaviour of the child; we need to cross-check our observations so that what we think we see is indeed as true a picture of events as possible; and we need to work with a terminology that assists communication and does not prejudice further constructive intervention on behalf of the child. In short, and in effect, we begin at once to reduce residual tension.

## DEALING WITH ANXIETY

There has now developed a vast literature on the subject of behavioural approaches to children, usually identified by titles which refer to behaviour 'modification' or 'management' or 'therapy'. Handbooks, such as those edited by Hersen and Bellack or by Leitenberg (1976), provide a wealth of information concerning all ages; they cover a vast assortment of conduct disorders and learning difficulties, and consistently support behavioural principles. They emphasise the need to observe carefully the actual behaviour of the child, and discourage the use of any terminology that is open to misinterpretation. The reader is urged to challenge all assumptions and to work towards and with observable facts, to clarify and refine all perceptions, resisting the vague in favour of the particular.

The assumption that 'he is a pain in the neck' suggests something other than 'he is sensitive', but when both represent the same behaviour seen from different viewpoints it helps to clarify just what the boy has done that others perceive so differently. Let us suppose that he has been complaining consistently to teacher and to parent that he is the victim of malicious teasing. The teacher, reckoning the boy asks for all he gets, is irritated by his incessant whimpering. The parent, believing the boy to be a budding Mozart, sees other boys as coarse and uncomprehending. As they stand, these differing perceptions are probably irreconcilable but agreement and effective follow-up will become possible once the anxiety in each camp has been de-fused. What is required is that both parties stand back, observe, take note of what is actually happening and then compare in objective terms their respective views of what this boy is doing. And note that the emphasis is on what the boy does rather than what he is. It is always unlikely that there will be agreement regarding the latter, but as to what the boy does and is seen to be doing, consensus is much more probable. In this case evidence is available that the boy prefers the piano to football, that he usually expresses this preference to his peers in words and manner offensive to them, and that they retaliate as often and as hurtfully as they can. The words and actions whereby the preference and the retaliation are expressed can be recorded literally, and new responses taught. The behaviours to be changed can be made explicit, so that not only boy and peer group, but also parent and teacher, will be left with little reason to doubt each other's assessment of the situation. For when behaviours are identified in non-judgmental terms, when people actually count for how long they last or how often they occur, behaviours then are seen as less troublesome and create less anxiety.

Integral to this kind of approach to the behaviour problems of children is the idea that behaviours which are the most amenable to change should be the first priority for changing. In other words, start at the beginning with the simplest task. The boy referred to above will first have to learn to smile and say hello, before he is ever ready to handle the hurt and frustration which drives him to run complaining to parent or teacher. So, in the field of anxiety management, the behaviours most amenable to change are those which involve least anxiety.

A practical strategy then is to draw up a priority list of those anxieties which need to be tackled. Start with the least anxiety-provoking situation and graduate through, up to say, ten steps to the situation of greatest anxiety to the child. As the child is encouraged to bring to bear his relaxation training to each stage in the anxiety hierarchy, so is the anxiety progressively de-fused. Child and caring adult become progressively 'desensitised' to the anxiety previously inherent in such situations. They feel better about them.

Let's look more carefully at this idea of an anxiety hierarchy, relating it to a child whom you know.

Consider a child who exhibits anxiety in different degrees and in different situations. What are those situations which generate anxiety? These can be considered as the backcloth to your child's anxious behaviour and should be the subject of discussion between you; do not assume that you know what is worrying your child without asking him.

Now examine how this anxiety is expressed. What does the child actually do in response to anxiety-provocation? Observe meticulously the reactions which appear under stress; for how long do they last and how frequently does each response occur?

Thirdly, taking each situation in turn and the child's response to it, together with the child look hard at the consequences of that response. What are the effects of anxious behaviour? Is this the outcome child or caring adult would have wished?

Draw up three parallel, corresponding columns, not too lengthy, covering from about five to ten significant issues, building the hierarchy from least to most anxious. The first (a) lists anxious situations for the child; the second (b) the behaviours corresponding to those situations; and the third (c) points out the effects of those behaviours (see Table 5.1).

Try this exercise yourself. Involve child, and where possible family members or working colleagues. Take your time and resolve to be totally honest. Record in three parallel columns so that the sequence from (a) to (b) to (c) can be understood and undisputed. What do you learn?

When information is presented in a model such as the above it is manageable to all concerned. This realisation itself helps reduce anxiety. Typically, the adult *in loco parentis* is by this stage less anxious and begins to transmit less worry and defeat to the child, more confidence and hope. Precisely now, when there is some positive momentum towards constructive solutions, is the time the child needs to call upon relaxation skills.

Usually the child who has learned to respond habitually with anxiety-laden behaviour will need to have received some measure of training in how to relax the different muscle groups, and to experience the difference between feeling tense and feeling relaxed. A range of

**Table 5.1:** Example of situation — response — effects list

| (a) Anxiety-provoking situations (the backcloth) | (b) Child's observed responses (actual behaviour corresponding to the situations listed) | (c) Effects of child's behaviour |
|---|---|---|
| 1. parents leave house without child . . . | 1. hides self, cries, throw things . . . | 1. parents leave anyway and punish child on return . . . |
| 2. going to bed alone, landing-light on . . . | 2. calls repeatedly for company, cries . . . | 2. disturbs household, late to sleep and therefore to rise next day . . . |
| 3. leaving home accompanied to visit shop . . . | 3. bites nails, clings to adult . . . | 3. friends pour scorn on child, shopping takes longer . . . |
| 4. leaving home alone to visit shop . . . | 4. leaves only under protest, swears, throws stones at window . . . | 4. shopping never done, return trip required . . . |
| 5. going to bed alone, light off . . . | 5. screams for bouts of 5 to 15 minutes duration, wets bed . . . | 5. disturbs house, late to sleep and to rise, bed to change . . . |
| 6. going to school . . . | 6. screams, swears, throws things when leaving house, demands adult company . . . | 6. draws attention of neighbourhood, makes mother late for her work . . . |
| 7. going to school on a Games day . . . | 7. screams, etc., wets self four days out of five, eats no breakfast . . . | 7. draws adverse attention, mum late, derision of classmates, hungry all morning . . . |

appropriate tense-and-relax exercises was given in Chapter 1. Further ideas for relaxation, which can be taught formally, are presented in Chapter 9.

Successful application of any relaxation training is a matter of recognising tension as it develops in the body, but instead of feeding it or allowing it to escalate, combating it with the (new) relaxed response. So what the child is to be encouraged to do is to apply suitable relaxation skills, whether acquired formally or through relatively informal counselling, to the situation which is known to be associated with anxiety.

The preferred therapeutic intervention proceeds as follows. The child, having previously been taught to relax, rehearses relaxation and is then reintroduced to the anxiety hierarchy, starting at the bottom of the anxiety scale. In a relaxed state the child is asked to imagine situation 1 (e.g. being left at home by parents). Reminded of his usual response (cries, hides away), the child is required to imagine what form a more relaxed response would take, and to visualise a more positive outcome (than waiting for parents to return home to punish him!). A similar exercise in imagery might be introduced soon afterwards, referring now to situation 2, the next step up the hierarchy. This could be to encourage the belief that more relaxed responses could at least be possible and help dissipate anxiety in a variety of situations, so leading to more positive, acceptable outcomes and effective solutions. The crucial test: the child having rehearsed situation 1 now takes it on in real life.

In this way each situation is rehearsed (imagined in a relaxed state) before being tackled in reality. Easier situations precede more difficult ones. The reinforcement at each stage carries child and adult more confidently and expectantly to the next.


## PERSISTENT ANXIETY

Amongst the more common childhood behaviour problems, where environmental and circumstantial factors are conducive to positive change, and where the child's most significant relationships are secure and healthy, anxieties tend to be acute rather than chronic and lend themselves readily to amelioration wiith general beneficial results. But when anxiety is the habitual response to certain situations or events, as in the more complex behaviour 'disorders', the child's response pattern can be explosive. Often it is as though behaviour 'steps off' the 'tense . . . relaxed' continuum into chaos. The child's conduct then has a crippling, negative effect on his life and on the lives of those around the child. In such cases anxiety has to be de-fused as part of the overall strategy to restore order and to develop a more positive lifestyle.

To help illustrate this point we could look in a little detail at a couple of case studies.

> Paul is 14 and attends a comprehensive secondary school two miles from home. His local school adjoins his home and that is where he would wish to attend, but his parents have chosen for him the school across town, since this more closely represents their ideal of the academic excellence they want for their son. Paul dislikes the estrangement of attending the school not attended by the boys who live near him. He dislikes having to cycle through the traffic to and from school four times daily, for his parents want him home each day for lunch. Moreover, he is not at all academically inclined: so he has been labelled 'dyslexic'; and he is withdrawn from Science and Games, which he likes and at which he excels, most days for remedial help. His parents pay for extra tuition two evenings a week at home and now feel they have done everything they can to give him special attention. He wants to please them but hates being 'made special'.
>
> The lad chews at his fingers habitually, he hates school but attends, and he smokes at every opportunity. He is constantly on edge lest his schoolwork should not improve and his smoking be discovered. Whenever he leaves the house in the evening he is told to return by some preordained early hour in order to catch up on his lessons. Out of doors he is restless, panics to be home on time, and is more often than not late. Then he has to explain himself to mum who always promises to relay the message of his latecoming to dad when he comes in. So he has to wait in trepidation for a second dressing down and further sanctions on his time and his adolescent wishes.
>
> The situation is complicated by the boy's failings and his parents' aspirations. Both parties are understandably anxious. The parents are counselled about their concerns and asked to compromise to accommodate their son's anxieties. His worries range from cycling home each evening (lowest rung on the anxiety ladder) to arriving home later than his limit (top of the scale). About mid-way is his anxiety about being singled out for remedial teaching. Parents refuse yet to transfer him to his local school but concede that he can do without all remedial help for the next six months, during which time he is instead to

follow a programme of guided reading under the supervision
of his English teacher and to undertake relaxation training at
the hands of the school's educational psychologist. Mum agrees
to assist with helping him read for pleasure and for
information, and to learn with him the relaxation exercises.

In due course Paul and his mother both adopt more relaxed
responses to the hitherto anxiety-provoking situations which
afflicted them. Father experiences a less tense household and he
develops a more easy-going attitude. Paul's reading and school-
work gradually become meaningful and important to him, since
this part of his life is no longer fraught with such anxiety, and he
at last pleases his parents in something. He also comes to terms
with the understanding that his parents want only the best for
him, so he no longer minds the fact that he journeys to school.
And although he does still smoke cigarettes and chew at his fingers, he does so out of habit and feels not at all anxious about it!

One point which will not have escaped the reader is the extent to which
relaxation training gives control to the trainee. This raises mighty implications for adult and child alike. The point will be made again, notably in
the sections referring to cerebral palsied children, and we will be considering the matter more fully in Chapter 8, 'Matters Arising'. So far,
the anxious subject has been characterised as 'out-of-control'; but
situations can arise where controlling influences need to be broken —
as in the case below.

Joanne, at 16 years of age, is very intelligent and bright, artistic
and academically ambitious. Anxiety management in her case
assumes subtleties and significance of an alarming, even sinister,
character. Her brother, two years younger, is if anything more
talented with a series of remarkable sporting and academic feats
to his credit. Both parents have proven successful in their respective professions and are settled with the chidren in their country
home after almost 20 years of marriage, obviously well-to-do
and satisfied with their lot. Theirs is a comfortable existence
indeed. Now to enjoy watching first Joanne then her brother
outshine all opposition, in all fields of endeavour to go from
success to success!

Subtly at first, then in the months immediately preceding
her O-levels, more palpably the pressure grows on Joanne.
Sensitive to her parents' expectations, and increasingly aware
of her responsibilities to schoolfriends and teachers, Joanne

develops anorexia. In the summer she sits her exams, she stands five feet eight inches tall and weighs just over six stone. During the months which follow she is in and out of hospital, her body weight varying dramatically as she alternates between overeating, a healthy diet and undernourishment.

For all to see, she is now very much in control. Whatever anyone else wants for her, she is in the driving seat herself and is inclined to steer a hair-raising course which serves to remind parents, teachers, doctors and others just who is boss. Her anorexia enables her to maintain her hold on those closest to her who reinforce her anorexic behaviour by the support they give her. But she is in a double-bind situation: if she carries on under-weight she risks losing weight further and becoming fatally ill, but meanwhile enjoys the comfort, consolation and release from all pressure to do well from her family and others; if she returns to a normal diet her health and general well-being will improve, but she must then expect everyone to demand excellence from her again; and what is more, the longer she postpones a return to normality, the louder those demands will be.

At first what Joanne sees is that she has assumed control over matters of consequence but at the price of serious weight loss. Quickly then she learns to control her weight loss too, such that she digests just enough to prevent irreversible damange. One day, however, she collapses and is rushed to hospital. The episode scares her and she seeks help — for this is the first time she feels anxiety about her conduct. In the therapy which ensues she perceives matters in terms of the double-bind described above, her anxiety is heightened and she is persuaded to do something to help herself. The final point, that people's demands of her will increase the longer she delays a return to normal, is a shell-shock to her.

Joanne learns a relaxation technique, ostensibly to be used to help cope with any anxieties which might be associated with eating. But there are none associated with eating; on the contrary as it transpires, food, its preparation for and consumption by others, become the mainstay of her being. Now, however, she can apply her well-developed relaxation skills in the light of the dawning realisation of the double-bind in her life. Anorexia she had seen as a heaven-sent means of wresting from others the control they seemed to hold over her. Now it becomes the source of a host of anxieties. As she begins to eliminate her anxiety through her own efforts and the understanding of her family, she begins to control the anorexia and reason returns to her life.

# 6

## The Cerebral Palsied Child

*Cerebral palsied children are indeed able to learn to relax. Relaxation training, applied to these children, is given its most severe testing.*

As educational psychologists both the authors have a broad generic role, with a range of responsibilities mainly but not exclusively concerned with school-age children with special educational needs. Within such a framework it is possible to explore and develop how an idea or practice might generalise from one situation to another, or from a restricted to a wider field. Not surprisingly therefore, the suggestion has evolved that relaxation training and its application might have real relevance as an educational aid to an even greater audience.

As a means of, or aid towards, therapy, relaxation technique is and has for many years been used by professionally trained therapists in the cause of remedial medicine — as part of the 'cure' process. As a preventive measure it has enjoyed a mixed reception and continues to be appraised with scepticism in some quarters. The value of relaxation training as a bona-fide educational tool may best be described as in the exploratory stage, but the evidence is growing in support of its claims. Its significance as an aid to learning, which can be therapeutic and/or educational, is the subject of this chapter. The shift in context — to the cerebral palsied child — should highlight the relevance and the possibilities of relaxation training.

### RATIONALE

To recap on some points made in earlier chapters: 'tension' and 'relaxation' may be represented on a continuum which is relatively neutral, allowing more objective evaluation of child and behaviour; 'tension' is common, useful and indeed necessary unless it develops in an extreme form such as 'anxiety'; in which form it may be 'de-fused' through relaxation training and its appropriate application.

Examples so far quoted have dealt with children whose difficulties and needs have nevertheless not prevented their continuing attendance in mainstream education. Indeed it has often been with the intention and the effect of enabling pupils to retain their position in the ordinary school that relaxation training has been used. The authors' experience has been that relaxation training has nearly always proven successful in this aim, or at the very least has been part of a general successful strategy. Where it has been less successful, the reasons identified have tended to fall into one of three categories. It could be that the necessary skills have not been adequately taught and therefore learned. More often it might be that the skills learned have not been applied sufficiently or appropriately. But the most common explanation is that there have been overriding considerations or factors, such as breakdown in the home situation, which have at least temporarily obstructed constructive intervention.

Pursuing this line of thought, two broad conclusions present themselves: uses of relaxation training need to be explored further, the technique modified and sharpened and applied more vigilantly, the revised methodology put to the test in a variety of situations and in extreme cases; alternatively, relaxation training is inadequate to the task. The latter proposition may be valid when this particular educational aid or form of therapy can do little or nothing to alter the circumstances which have caused the child to become excessively tense in the first place. Thus, if a child is anxious at the prospect of his parents separating, or at an imminent court appearance or imposed stay in hospital, then relaxation training may be helpful in enabling the child to come to terms with the event, but is usually very unlikely to prevent its occurrence. In other words, where the prevailing situation is *in extremis* and out of the child's control, time does tend to be the only healer. Then the 'therapist' — whoever that is, and it is often the child himself — has to judge carefully and knowingly the moment to concentrate predominantly, perhaps exclusively, on self to begin to work on solutions to the problem as he sees it.

The other conclusion — that relaxation technique might be modified and applied in extreme cases — is just as demanding, not so much of fine judgments and of a coming to terms with huge odds, but of the need to re-evaluate and question old assumptions, to be willing to innovate and to research new fields. Partly in response to this challenge, partly out of concern for the children themselves, we have tried to address some of the problems facing cerebral palsied (CP) children.

It is not within the scope of this book to enter into detailed consideration of the subject of cerebral palsy, and it is assumed that the reader is familiar with, or has a working knowledge of, the condition. The available literature typifies the CP child as either spastic, athetoid, ataxic or flaccid (floppy) and the condition is usually classified under three categories: medical, educational and welfare. The local library is unlikely to carry much material but can order from central stock or specialist sources, such as a university or college library, while the best source of practical advice and reading matter continues to be the Spastics Society. Publications, such as Finnie's *Handling the young cerebral palsied child at home* (1968), are informative and very readable.

For the present purposes it should suffice to acknowledge that the CP person has to deal with a range of disabling movements which handicap any attempt to effect physical motor co-ordination, and to exert control over the total environment, including the personal, the social and the physical world round about. Cerebral palsy exists in a great many forms and to different extents, but consistent across types and cases are difficulties of control over one's own movements and over the immediate environment. Even in those cases where low muscle-tone predominates, as with the typically floppy child, a greater measure of control can be effected if a greater degree of tension is actually induced.

Physiotherapy can assist someone with CP to accommodate the handicap and to make best use of the bodily functions available. Therapeutic aids, including those dependent on computer technology, provide help or provide access to that which might not otherwise be accessible. They are a physical adjunct to the disablement, a prop or a tool to help someone cope better.

It is not intended here to attempt to argue for any other aid or technique to take the place of efficient physiotherapy. Relaxation training, however, might very well complement physiotherapy, and in any event is applicable in those situations where physiotherapy is perhaps unavailable or inappropriate. The CP child in the classroom about to tackle a pencil-and-paper exercise, or take a stab at a jigsaw, cannot often call upon a physiotherapist there and then to assist. But if that child can apply previously learned relaxation skills to the business of undertaking a physically demanding task, then those skills and the process of learning them can justifiably be said to operate as an educational aid. Alternatively, the teacher or parent, for instance, with a confident grasp of relaxation practices, may in such circumstances be able to prepare the child for the task ahead. It is not too difficult to imagine a scenario where first the task is set out in a manageable form for the child; secondly, the child is given a reminder or cue to relax; and then the task is undertaken with less hindrance from the disablement.

Exploring the possibilities of teaching relaxation skills to young CP children, and of trying to employ the new skills usefully, is one way of testing out relaxation training and application under the severest of circumstances. More to the point, it does at the same time offer an opportunity for disabled children to develop valuable, enabling skills such that they may become more active participants in life around them.

## CEREBRAL PALSY AND ANXIETY

The analogy with the anxious child now becomes more and more persuasive. When considered in purely functional terms, spasticity is characterised by acute and also chronic tension in certain muscle groups. So too is anxiety. Anxiety can resemble the usual form of cerebral palsy, in that it involves difficulties of control over one's own actions and over the immediate environment. Both can be depicted as debilitating conditions 'found' at the same extreme of the 'tension . . . relaxation' continuum. The CP children referred to in the following pages are not being portrayed as anxious or having an anxiety-related disorder, but to the extent that their muscles and limbs tighten up in immediate response to given situations, despite what they want to happen or want to do, then theirs is a predicament analogous to that faced by anxious children. By concentrating on the points of similarity, rather than the obvious differences between the two populations, reciprocal benefits to both types of child might be forthcoming. As was suggested earlier, the so-called floppy child is not necessarily excepted from such benefits. All CP children need to become aware of the degree of tension present in their limbs so that they can begin to exert more control over their own bodies and consequently over the environment in which they find themselves.

Originally, the authors were interested in determining whether biofeedback could be of use to CP children. The work of Ann Harrison (1975, Chapter 7) had indicated that CP adults could make use of the information provided by biofeedback instruments to gain a greater measure of control over their own muscle activity. The Harrison study concerned adults diagnosed as CP but without any other known major disability. No comparable information existed in respect of CP children.

Indeed, the children to whom we as school psychologists were asked to give priority, comprised a multiple-handicap group who not only had CP but also had no effective means of communication. Moreover, as far as could be assessed two, possibly three, of the children would be of 'average' or above intellect; the remaining nine or ten were decidedly limited, some severely impaired in all areas of ability. A hard core of five presenting an astonishing array of handicapping conditions would in due course become the principal focus of study. The attraction of this group was that their needs were so powerful and the means to help them apparently so weak.

According to the teaching staff closest to, and most knowledgeable of, the situation, a significant skill for these children to learn would be to point accurately at certain defined targets. The children were all about seven years of age, with extraordinarily frustrating difficulties of mobility and communication associated with their spastic quadriplegia, who had all been thus afflicted since birth and were now attending a school for physically handicapped children. Since none of the children could express themselves in speech or by gesture in any way that was consistently recognisable, their teachers tried to help them communicate by means of Blissymbols (whereby familiar people, objects, situations and ideas are depicted in simple, graphic form on a chart presented to the child). One major problem for these children was to point to their chosen symbol on the chart before them. Manoeuvring the trunk into a position to address the table appropriately, bringing the shoulder and arm into line with the selected section of the chart and struggling to maintain eye contact with the symbol whilst at the same time to distend an habitually crooked finger was a frustrating, often harrowing experience — to witness let alone to undergo! The process of targeting a Blissymbol was not unlike a range of tasks undertaken daily at home, school and elsewhere, and yet it presented enormous difficulties. So too must that range of other tasks!

It soon became obvious that the harder the child tried to point to the chosen target and the more frustrated he grew with not communicating the ideas intended, then the more the effort to point and so to communicate became hampered and obstructed by involuntary muscle movements. So, for instance, the little girl urgently striving to locate the symbol 'toilet' on her Bliss matrix, might try to point with the right forefinger. But the elbow of her right arm would persist in getting lodged in the crook of her wheelchair. Her other arm

79

and both legs would meanwhile thrash around in spasm, upsetting the table, colliding with all manner of environmental hazards. The girl's neck muscles would be pulling her head to one side, making eye contact with the target area progressively more awkward and less reliable. For all her efforts the child was actually punished, since rarely was she successful in her aim and her poor limbs would collect an assortment of self-inflicted bruises. Indeed, it seemed the more powerful her motivation, the less likely was she to succeed.

This is a distressingly familiar state of affairs for CP children themselves and for all those who care for them. Not unlike the development of the panic reaction described in an earlier chapter, here was a situation where the tension response spiralled into something uncontrollable and destructive.

## PRESENTATION OF EXPERIMENTAL TASKS

It was decided then to present this age group of CP children who were without an effective means of communication, and so were engaged at school in the Bliss programme, with a range of carefully constructed tasks considered well within their estimated ability. Each activity involved the critical task of targeting, using the preferred hand. The children's responses were timed, video-recorded and noted. Attempts using the non-preferred hand were then recorded in the same way. The results were plain to see: while the children varied to some extent in their success rate and with one hand rather than the other, even the simplest of tasks was impeded by the uncontrolled, irrelevant activity of the other limbs.

In order therefore to provide each child with information about what the non-involved limbs were doing during the targeting task, biofeedback instruments were introduced. Initially each child was given experience of the instrument without having to tackle any task at all. They each quickly learned that by relaxing a given limb the 'machine' would register less noise and the needle on its display would show clearly a drop towards zero. Often each child would fashion an individual technique of creating the required relaxed response, reflecting the CP characteristic whereby the limb may be set or held in an abnormal or distorted position because that is how it feels most comfortable. Biofeedback helped make each child more aware of the involuntary and relatively useless movement in the limbs supposedly at rest, and now each was able to demonstrate some measure of control over this extraneous, involuntary activity.

Now too, instead of exhorting the children to 'do their best' or 'try hard', all conditions and circumstances were deliberately relaxed and the children soothed into their most relaxed posture and attitude. In this more relaxed situation each child performed more successfully at the targeting tasks. Not surprisingly these relaxed and successful sessions proved very popular with the children themselves. The setting conditions most favourable to least tension for the child were established gradually throughout the course of these various training sessions. Of considerable significance were that the immediate environment was relatively distraction-free and that in this setting each child was made comfortable and subject to no pressure. Furthermore, the child did not have to compete with anyone to share the available adult attention, which was consistently geared to reinforcing the suggestion that calm and relaxation would surely achieve desired ends for the child.

**Figure 6.1:** An electromyograph biofeedback instrument in use with the electrodes attached to the forearm. The trainee is attempting to keep the muscles in the right forearm inactive whilst pressing the buzzer key with her left hand.

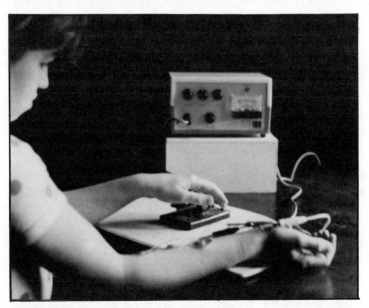

These are not conditions which are typical of the classroom even in the friendliest, most caring school. Children do have to compete and share; schools and elsewhere do contain distractions and pressures. Yet under optimum conditions here was evidence of correlation between relaxed muscles and success at motor tasks, previously a source of failure for all these young CP children. The range of difficulties of motor control experienced by the children persuaded their teachers to discontinue the Bliss programme, so the requirement of the children to target with the minimum of error began to receive less emphasis. What would continue, however, to predominate for teaching purposes would be the requirement placed on children to undertake a great range of tasks, *which they might achieve* if suitably relaxed, and at which they would surely fail if not.

---

*Relaxed?*

There appears to be considerable scope for confusion, given the more colloquial usage of this word. 'Relaxed' often suggests an appearance or presentation of calm and imperturbability, which is what the observer wants to see or is persuaded to see; this is reassuring, comforting, in line with some previously conceived notion of what is, and may have more to do with innocent prejudice than considered judgment or the facts of the situation. A singer may be said to have a relaxed singing style, a golfer a relaxed swing, a sprinter a relaxed stride, or an occasion may be described as relaxed because no-one has dressed ostentatiously for it. Appearances are inevitably deceptive.

Billy's parents and teacher are asked: under what circumstances is he at his most relaxed during the day? They agree it is when he is lying on a carpet surrounded by his 'favourite' toys: Dinky cars, trucks and buses. Billy's mum and dad perceive him as relaxed because his immediate surroundings are their choice of home comforts and because his face expresses evident pleasure whenever these particular toys are brought to his notice. Taking her lead from his parents, the teacher seeks to replicate such conditions whenever she wants to relax Billy at school, by which she means provide him with some form of non-academic, undemanding diversion.

But this little boy, as matters stand, cannot take advantage of this supposedly rewarding situation. He doesn't know how to relax here and no-one has thought to teach him. Billy is intent on grasping a hand-sized London Transport double-decker bus. The intention is enough to stimulate tension in

---

his limbs to the extent that his activity becomes athetoid. Gross, stiff, jerking, inaccurate movement is his lot. He knocks the bus over and eventually out of reach. His 'free' hand inadvertently hooks a finger in a car window. Billy rolls on to this hand trapping finger and hand with the car. Always it is merely a matter of time before the child has to be rescued . . . from a relaxing activity!

Some time later, Billy sits supported in his chair. Before him stands a table, its position and height adjusted to his requirements, and on the table there is a bell to press when he is given the word. His arm is restrained and his hand held by the instructor who releases them when he tells the boy to press the bell. The object of the exercise has been to study how Billy would undertake this simple targeting task. However, what assumes greater significance is Billy's response to the physical contact with the instructor. For, after only a few trials the instructor has become more sensitive to the tension in Billy's arm and hand, and now instead of just restraining them he is actually gently massaging the muscles and rotating Billy's wrist. The child visibly relaxes. Altogether less rigid in his chair, his neck and shoulders ease, allowing his arms to come to rest on his lap. One arm is still in contact with the instructor but no longer is it being actively manipulated. Billy bends this arm in the direction of the adult's breast pocket, and receives encouragement to discover what is inside. His response is to reach further, and although his hand and arm are not without tension, they are sufficiently so that he can slip his hand into the pocket. Triumphant grin! Throughout this little incident the atmosphere is subdued, at times almost soporific, yet Billy remains remarkably aware and interested in all around him.

The environment has held little in the way of pressure or distraction and the child has received the undivided attention of the two psychologists present. Not in any preordained fashion but very subtly indeed, concentration is transferred from the task itself to creating and maintaining conditions of optimum relaxation. Billy has let it be known that, however useful targeting might be for him, the more significant skill is that he be able to relax.

To relax or to be relaxed becomes something more than a passive reaction, happening usually after some form of activity. For it can itself be active, in that it requires attention and practice to achieve proficiency; in other words, to be able to relax is a skill which is needed before rather than after a task is tackled; it is the prelude to rather than the result of another activity. Those people, situations, etc., we perceive as relaxed are associated inevitably with high-quality performance; a lot of training has gone into that relaxed performance.

So Billy is given extensive experience in relaxing himself. One day he returns mid-morning to his classroom, wheels his chair up to his table and is told to resume the task he left earlier. A series of crashes and collisions announce his difficulties just in getting set in position to start his work. His teacher says simply, 'Billy! Relax.' The lad stops in his tracks, removes his hands from the wheelchair, takes a few moments to bring his arms and legs to rest, breathes deeply for a few seconds, looks from side to side. Then very deliberately . . . almost gingerly, he moves one wheel just a quarter-turn . . . then the other . . . until he is satisfied with his position relative to the table. Now he can give his attention to his task, and he does so quite cheerfully. The child is relaxed: the task can be done.

## CONCLUSIONS AND DISCUSSION

Amongst the questions presenting themselves at this point were those relevant to the validity of the 'experiment' with the CP children, and how reliable was the information being collated. But it has not yet been possible to work towards a more sharply defined, controlled experimental model, even if any such model had ever been conceptualised, so the essentially theoretical questions have not yet been pursued. More practical demands have taken precedence. These raise mundane but critical issues such as whether or not the relaxation skills which can be learned under optimum conditions may be learned equally when circumstances are less favourable; whether indeed they might be consolidated for longer if learned at home rather than at school; and, if these skills really are to be useful, how to ensure they will be applied in those situations where most needed. Each child therefore became an experiment in his own right, the essential question being: how can this child transfer relaxation skills from a comfortable situation to a much more demanding one?

Certainly the relaxation skills being taught posed no problem for these CP children. Having had much experience of the concepts of tension and relaxation, they were able to understand and follow the simple procedure laid out, and interpretation was in accordance with the individual's abilities and needs. Indeed these were often old skills which the children were being asked to recall and use, but in new circumstances. Relaxation was now being offered as an antidote to tension and as something subject to the child's own control rather than someone else's (who may or may not make it available at any given time). It was being given a place in the experience as well as in the vocabulary of the child; it was given a meaning.

When asked to concentrate entirely on relaxing particular muscle groups, the children proved able to demonstrate a measure of control hitherto considered impossible. Their parents were surprised, and the professionals involved were surprised, indeed suspicious. But the biofeedback records over many months and the video-recordings of the children in a variety of activities and situations were evidence of the CP child being much more in control, and being ready and able to learn greater control.

We can speculate regarding some of the reasons for this hitherto unsuspected measure of control. In the first place, the professionals involved with the CP child, and those directly influential on the child's parents, do tend to support the view, unwittingly or not, that so major a handicap as CP is not only limiting but also largely immutable. A number of assumptions operate: that the child cannot do something, and what is more, cannot *ever* do it; that the condition is a permanent disablement, a disease without a cure; that the sufferer will adjust well or ill to it; that advances in medicine or technology or education or welfare will principally serve to assist this process of adjustment; and that expectations should remain low. This is to see the problem only from the outside in. But there is another form of explanation offered by the use of biofeedback, which does of course provide powerful, experiential evidence to the user. Anyone who uses a biofeedback instrument receives first-hand information through the device of certain physiological reactions, as that person's body responds to external stimuli. To the CP person used to being the recipient of other people's interpretation of events for and about him, the information of the machine, individually calibrated, is uniquely personal and persuasive. Furthermore, it provides strong motivation — namely, that even more control than that already achieved is possible. So long as the biofeedback information continues to support the hypothesis that relaxation of the muscles is associated with greater control of them, it reinforces the feeling of well-being experienced by the user. If the information is that the user is losing control, then the person well-versed and practised in relaxation training is equipped to self-induce a greater degree of relaxation in the knowledge that this in turn will revert the trend and the instrument will once again inform that control is returning to the user. Relaxation then is, and is perceived by its user to be, the opposite of or antidote to tension; but critically, it enables other 'goodies' to follow. It is surely the CP child's motivation to effect change coupled with the panoply of relaxation skills which produces the greater measure of control referred to. It is a sobering thought that maybe the child's motivation to effect change is a good deal more potent than that of the parent or professional.

What then are the implications? One is that there are educational advantages at least, in taking the approach to CP, as to other forms of severe learning disability, that the person concerned is not 'abnormal' or 'less than normal'; rather that the movement and range of movement of the CP person is qualitatively different. By this it is implied that some control over the environment is not perforce ruled out, but that it can be at least partly enabled through the appropriate application of relaxation training. That such control may in fact be enabled implies a teaching programme, a willingness and ability to teach and to learn, and by everyone, not just by professional people, a very significant acknowledgement — namely, that humanitarian considerations can be more sensitive than the clinician's appraisal; and that what the afflicted individual feels, thinks, or can do about the affliction is important in providing a sense of worth and purpose in life. Like the anxious child, the CP child can gain a foothold on the road to rehabilitation, and the help required is the help given for the purposes of helping oneself. Again what is implied is that less is to be done *to* the child (or adult), more to be done to create the conditions promoting relaxation, self-awareness and sufficiency and constructive solutions to persistent difficulties wherever they may be found.

Accordingly, this seminal, exploratory work with the CP children now entered a new phase. Two avenues seemed readily to open: the first, where the parents would take their children through relaxation activities at home on a regular basis; and the other, to help each child to relax when needed by means of a 'cue' which would trigger the relaxation response. Such a cue could be either self-induced, the effect being that the child 'tells' himself to relax, or it might be used by a third party to 'remind' the child to relax (recall the anecdote about Billy who was told, 'Relax'). The idea of a self-induced cue is especially appealing since it could be particularly forceful in providing the child with autonomy of control. Both ideas will be pursued more fully in a later chapter, but some of the early attempts, their advantages and disadvantages, particularly with regard to home-based relaxation training, need touching upon here.

It is common practice to give initial training in relaxation procedures through counselling or therapeutic interviews, then to provide the trainee with an audio-cassette of the same whereby the skills can be reinforced at home. With the CP children their parents' aid was enlisted on two counts: to ensure that each child had a good, working grasp of the terms, 'relax' and 'tense', and the conception that one was at odds with the other; and to guide and support the child to relax under instruction. All the parents had given their support to the psychologists' efforts and now were fully briefed before each home was equipped with recording charts and the following notes of guidance:

---

**Relaxation training**

name . . . . . .
d.o.b. . . . . . . date . . . . .

The first exercises we want you to undertake with your child comprise two sets of activities:
A. the 'tense' and 'relax' game; and
B. the relaxation cassette.
You are advised to set a daily pattern, finding say half-an-hour each morning and each afternoon for each set of activities.

*A. The 'tense' and 'relax' game*

1. Explain the terms, 'tense' and 'relax', and use them as often as possible.
2. Support your child on the floor with cushions, etc., such that each limb can be free.
3. You squat immediately in front.
4. Tell child to 'tense' right arm by pressing hard against your hands . . . you resist rather than push back.
5. When you feel child's pressure, tell child to 'relax' by no longer pressing against you.
6. Repeat for right arm, five times in succession.
7. Then repeat for each limb in turn.
8. Observe and record meticulously.
9. Please make a note of any modifications of the above you think would be useful for your child.

---

> ### B. Relaxation training (cassette)
>
> 1. If you had the floor game in the morning then leave this until late afternoon, again explaining what you are about and any unfamiliar terms.
> 2. Before introducing the child to the cassette, listen through all the instructions yourself, then choose somewhere for the child that is eminently comfortable and free from disturbance.
> 3. As above (A. 8 and 9), note your child's responses.
>
> *Footnote*: Please add any information you consider relevant — e.g. does your chid have a preferred hand? or leg? — is one side noticeably stronger than the other? — any difficulties encountered with either A or B?, etc.

The reader will note that relaxation training consists of a series of 'exercises'. This is in keeping with the philosophy that to relax is to engage in something active, which for the purposes of training is a deliberate response to the tension engendered in the muscles. Perhaps this was why some parents reported dificulty in fitting the exercises into a twice-daily schedule. They found their children after a long day at school to be too tired to relax! Bearing in mind these were extremely disabled young children, travelling long distances daily to and from school, they proved remarkably committed to the training schedule.

The cassette, on the other hand, concentrated heavily on the relaxation aspect. It asked the listener to follow a series of 'tense' and 'relax' instructions, but then to consolidate with some deep relaxation (only) recorded on the B side of the tape. The latter was reported as very popular with children and adults alike! One mother recollected a classic experience: tired dad home from work, goes up to small daughter's room to listen through the relaxation tape with her; some time later, mum hears child's voice: 'Mum! Dad has fallen asleep on the floor!' Relaxation is never reported as inducing sleep with the child, however, who has from the onset been encouraged to believe that to learn to relax has to involve active participation.

These early attempts to arrange for relaxation training to proceed at home under parent guidance met with qualified success. Any difficulties reported were on the parents' side: for many their own needs as the principal caring agents in their child's upbringing, with all that this involves, are not served substantially by having something else to do each day. Almost certainly, too, parents in these circumstances require support themselves, probably best from other parents who have had similar experiences first-hand. This is less true in the case of the parents of anxious children, but it is one factor in the argument to provide children themselves with their own strategy whereby to tackle their own problems through relaxation training.

Similarly, a training 'package' for teachers has not yet been devised to be as effective for application within the classroom. Difficulties arise in terms of curriculum method, and of school and classroom management. These are areas under investigation at the present time, and need not be discounted as insoluble problems. But clearly in the field of special education, let alone in mainstream schools, while the need to provide a relaxed atmosphere receives due attention, the requirement to teach relaxation skills to individuals does not.

This is not meant to convey a depressing picture. On the contrary, an essentially novel idea always takes some time to gain a foothold in education circles, and it is well that it is so. Typically, the conviction will grow that relaxation training is a viable proposition once more individual children have demonstrated they can benefit from it. Training ideas and 'packages', including the notion of the self-helping 'cue' for children, can be explored and pursued in different contexts. Currently, it would appear that the use of a cue to induce relaxation may well be a distinct methodology from the 'package' since it is relevant to the child in a very direct way, being unique and personal to the individual. Amongst all the variables which affect the child's learning processes and his self-respect, and which influence how he responds to the demands of life, the impact of relaxation training, its application and how it may be cued in at will, is impossible to measure. But the probability is that here is a most valuable and significant aid to the child in need.

# 7

# A Learning Framework

*A number of different concepts have been put forward to explain the development of anxiety. The approach adopted to bring about the alleviation of anxiety has been discussed. In this chapter an attempt is made to provide a theoretical rationale for the various processes involved.*

The first five chapters of this book served to set out the nature of the task which must be undertaken in helping children and young people to manage their own emotional responses. To the extent that this task is successfully achieved, children will be enabled to more efficiently cope with the vast range of potentially anxiety-provoking situations which they will undoubtedly meet during the course of their everyday lives. The sixth chapter dealt with the very special case of a group of extremely handicapped children who have been helped to gain some measure of control over the involuntary muscular spasms which so hinder their efforts to carry out the whole range of movement which most of us take for granted. In this chapter an attempt will be made to show how the knowledge gained through working with this group has been used to inform and refine the work that is being carried out with 'normal' children who are disabled by anxiety. A great many different strands have been revealed so far, all of which have contributed to the conviction that children can be given the means to successfully alleviate the problems which arise from anxiety.

## THE EXTREME CASE

It would be quite true to state that when the authors first became involved with the group of severely handicapped cerebral palsied children they regarded them as presenting quite different problems from those experienced by the children they treated in ordinary schools. When dealing with so-called 'normal' children the aim was to use some form of relaxation training right from the very first case. It was considered that a great deal of the behaviour which caused concern to parents and to teachers, and to the children themselves, was anxiety-related and would be amenable to change using relaxation techniques. In the case of the cerebral palsied group the assumption was made that the involuntary muscular spasms were caused by some malfunctioning of the nervous system which was completely out of the control of the child. The hope that some help could be given to these children arose from the idea which was held that amongst all the inappropriate messages that the muscles were receiving from the brain, which caused all the tensing and jerking, were some appropriate messages which the muscles were unable to recognise.

The situation could be likened to one where a listener is endeavouring to pick up a message from a radio receiver against a background of static interference and other competing transmissions. If the further difficulty was added that the listener did not know the nature of the message he was expected to receive and would, therefore, be unable to recognise it even when it came through against the background noise this would represent a fair approximation of the situation experienced by the cerebral palsied children. The one ray of hope which it was felt might exist in this seemingly intractable situation was that amongst all the noise and confusion the useful message might be hidden.

The first approach was to tackle this problem head on. The functional message was there amongst the mish-mash; our job was to give the children the means to recognise it. From reading the previous chapter it will be clear that this approach was at the same time too simple and too complex. Too simple because it took too little account of individual differences and the strategies that the children had already adopted to deal with their problems; too complex because it was only successful in dealing with discrete movements of individual limbs in single situations. The complexity would arise from the need to teach new strategies for every conceivable movement that the children would want to make. Their need was for a generalised approach that could be of use to them in all situations, whether these were completely new to them or repetitions of what had been done before.

There was also the problem of the initially adopted stance, common to most therapists who deal with handicapped people, that they are bodies to which something has to be done. The therapy is imposed from outside in the hope that it will eventually be internalised and come under the control of the person himself. This was quite the opposite of the approach already adopted when dealing with 'normal' children where the aim, from the beginning of any intervention, was to put the child back in control. Fortunately, these little 'non-communicating' children were finally able to get their message through that what was being done to them was too mechanical, too much associated with their specific handicap and not enough to do with their being people in their own right, with their own anxieties and their own emotions. When this insight was finally hammered home the whole thrust of the therapy was changed so that the emphasis was placed on the acquisition of relaxation techniques and a whole new range of possibilities opened up. These possibilities were seen as being applicable not only to the cerebral palsied group but to all children with anxiety-related problems.

With the adoption of this different orientation towards the difficulties experienced by the cerebral palsied group it soon became clear that the position on the 'tension . . . relaxation' continuum is of vital importance to their ability to control their limbs. The problem faced by such people is that anxiety is a learned response of enormous significance to them because, not surprisingly, they become anxious whenever they have to make a movement. There is the abiding uncertainty of whether they will manage it reasonably successfully or whether they will fail. This is a problem that non-handicapped people never, or only rarely, face. Yet it is a part of the fabric of everyday life for those with cerebral palsy. Their need to acquire a means of controlling their position on the 'tension . . . relaxation' continuum is related not only to controlling the anxiety level but also the tension in their muscles. That relaxation training gave them a means to do this represented a great breakthrough. Although much work remains to be done in order to devise ways by which this ability may be utilised in everyday life, the importance of the fact that the skill can be taught cannot be over-emphasised. From the point of view of dealing with the anxiety-related problems of ordinary children the breakthrough was just as significant. If cerebral palsied chldren can use relaxation techniques to help them deal with their enormous problems it would not be unreasonable to expect these techniques to be even more effective when used by children whose problems are far less extreme.

The need to pay very close attention to the nature of the environmental situation became paramount in helping these children. The task in which the child is engaged could be as simple as being dressed in his coat. In the current setting there is the physical environment, which includes the coat itself and its fastenings, the room where the dressing is taking place and the memory of past experiences with these things. Significant in the social environment is the person who is doing the dressing and the memories of past experiences with this person. In the personal environment are the memories of past experiences of discomfort, success or failure which attended this activity. In discussion with parents it soon became very clear that these simple everyday situations were the sources of great tension leading to anxiety and failure. The vicious circle of tension, anxiety and failure culminating in learned inappropriate responses and the confirmation of continued failure could almost be seen developing with relentless inevitability.

There is no doubt that it was through working with this little group of children that recognition first came about of the immense significance of the different aspects of the environment, past, present and future, in the learning of emotional responses. The model of emotional learning which will be constructed in the remainder of this chapter is based on the work carried out with 'normal' children and with those suffering from cerebral palsy. However, this model has much in common with the recent theories of emotion put forward by Izard (1972) and by Mandler (1976). Readers who would appreciate a much fuller theoretical treatment of this subject would find both these texts extremely valuable.

## THE 'NORMAL' CASE

All of us, during our normal everyday lives, are being continually confronted with a stream of situations to which we are obliged to react. Many of these situations will be near-repetitions of events which have occurred before, and the reactions made to them will also tend to repeat sequences of behaviour which have proved satisfactory in the past. However, even an experienced adult can expect to meet new situations from time to time but for a child such confrontations are everyday occurrences. A great deal of learning will come about as a result of this succession of new experiences, some of which will be obvious; the child learns to walk, to speak, to avoid danger, to master the skill of pedalling a tricycle and so on. Less obvious is the learning which takes place and contributes to the nature of the emotions he will associate with different situations.

The sources of this learning have been dealt with in earlier chapters along with the idea of the current position on the 'tension . . . relaxation' continuum being affected by past memories, the present situation and expectations for the future. The emotional response produced in any situation will come about as a consequence of the interaction of the various aspects of this highly complex system. Our knowledge of these interactive forces is at best incomplete, but it is possible to sketch in some outlines of a system which may help to illuminate the process.

It is possible to identify three main elements which contribute to the proposed system. By dealing with each of these separately, and also by showing the links between them, a better understanding of the development of emotional states may be achieved. The first major aspect of the system is the environment, past, present and future. Secondly there is the 'tension . . . relaxation' continuum, and thirdly there is the consequent emotional response.


## THE ENVIRONMENT

The aspects of the environment which are related to time, i.e. past, present and future, are significant for the child in the manner in which these aspects have been experienced at a personal level, a social level and a physical level. The significance of these environmental factors, the manner of their development and the learning associated with them is dealt with in some detail in Chapters 2 and 3. The purpose of referring to them again is to illustrate how interrelationships exist and how these may affect each other. The possibilities which exist for interaction can be seen in Figure 7.1. Applying the interactions suggested by the figure to a problem which was actually experienced by a child may assist in making the concept a little more clear.

Mark was experiencing problems both at school and at home, which appeared to be associated with bad temper, poor achievement and an inability to get on with his school fellows or his family. He was untidy, unkempt and sickly-looking. However, when he was seen in a non-threatening relaxed atmosphere he showed that he was quite capable intellectually and had a well-developed sense of humour. He was prepared to discuss his problems which he admitted to quite readily. He confessed to being very easily annoyed by quite trivial things but could see no way in which he could alter this. After some discussion a pattern began to emerge which suggested that the extreme irritability which he showed was possibly associated with chronic over-tiredness.

This proved to be a fruitful avenue for investigation when it transpired that Mark experienced great difficulty in getting to sleep each night, and that for as long as he could remember he always resorted to banging his head rhythmically on the pillow as a somewhat dubious aid to induce sleep.

Applying the suggested learning system to Mark's problems reveals

**Figure 7.1:** Learning system

| Child's environment | Current situation | | |
|---|---|---|---|
| | Past | Present | Anticipated |
| Personal | Arousal level. Associated emotional states with past arousal level. Genetic endowment, e.g. temperament. | Arousal level. Memory of emotional states at similar times. | Anticipation of what emotions will be felt, based upon memories of previously experienced similar situations. |
| Social | Peer group, e.g. classmates, friends. Family, e.g. siblings, parents, extended family. Significant adults, e.g. teachers, neighbours. Behaviour of these towards child. | Significant figures in current situation. Memory of how these behaved previously. | Significant figures expected in future environment and previous experience of them. Expected behaviour of these figures. |
| Physical | Home. School. Neighbourhood. Physical character of these, e.g. colour, sound, smell, furnishings. | Current physical environment. Experiences associated with current physical environment and memories of emotional associations. | Meaning of physical situation expected. Associated memories of such physical situations. |

some interesting possibilities. The current situation is that he cannot get to sleep. Considering his personal environment from the point of view of the past it can be assumed that it will contain learned experiences of a particular emotional state. This emotional state will also be associated with a particular level of arousal, i.e. a particular position on the 'tension . . . relaxation' continuum. His social environment will contain memories of the disapproval of his parents regarding his head-banging and this, too, will contribute to his current emotional state and likewise to a particular position on the 'tension . . . relaxation' continuum. His peer group contains his brother who sleeps in the same bedroom and also bangs his head. The past physical environment will be a virtual replica of that which he has confronted every night for as long as he can remember, and will have associated with it the knowledge of unsuccessfully trying to promote sleep, of repeated failure and frustration. Yet another contribution will accrue to Mark's emotional state and to the position on the 'tension . . . relaxation' continuum.

The anticipated outcome of the current situation will contain all these elements projected into the future. He will expect to experience certain emotional states associated with failure and frustration, he knows that he will bang his head, he expects his brother to do the same, he expects to incur the displeasure of his parents. The sights, the sounds, the physical atmosphere of his bedroom is not expected to be any different from what it was on hundreds of other occasions.

Mark lying in bed in the present is impinged upon by his experiences of the past and his expectations of the future, and it would be surprising if these factors did not affect the second stage of the system, the 'tension . . . relaxation' continuum.

## THE 'TENSION . . . RELAXATION' CONTINUUM

The resultant position on the 'tension . . . relaxation' continuum will depend upon the levels of arousal associated with the environmental factors referred to in Figure 7.1. It has been suggested elsewhere that a child may well feel at ease in a very threatening physical environment providing he is accompanied by an adult with whom he has learnt to feel confident. The environment is still threatening, and were the child to be left alone in it — or worse, in the company of an adult who is also associated with feelings of anxiety — the resultant position on the 'tension . . . relaxation' continuum would be entirely different.

Figure 7.2 attempts to show how such a system might work. Each aspect of the environment produces a level of arousal which is appropriate to the child's perception of its significance. This would not occur at a conscious level but would be an automatic response which has been learned due to past experiences. These separate arousal responses then combine together and average out to produce a level of arousal which is in turn associated with a particular position on the 'tension . . . relaxation' continuum. Only three environmental contributions are shown in the figure, but clearly the system could be much more complex than this.

Returning to our example of Mark it can now be seen how his experiences of the past, his knowledge of the present and his anticipation of the future can each make a separate contribution to his current level of arousal. This current level of arousal, which will, in effect, be an averaging out of the three different levels, will determine

**Figure 7.2**: Learning system

| Child's environment | Current situation | | |
|---|---|---|---|
| | Past | Present | Anticipated |
| Personal | Arousal level. Associated emotional states with past arousal level. Genetic endowment, e.g. temperament. | Arousal level. Memory of emotional states at similar times. | Anticipation of what emotions will be felt based upon memories of previously experienced similar situations. |
| Social | Peer group, e.g. classmates, friends. Family, e.g. siblings, parents, extended family. Significant adults, e.g. teachers, neighbours. Behaviour of these towards child. | Significant figures in current situation. Memory of how these behaved previously. | Significant figures expected in future environment and previous experience of them. Expected behaviour of these figures. |
| Physical | Home. School. Neighbourhood. Physical character of these, e.g. colour, sound, smell, furnishings. | Current physical environment. Experiences associated with current physical environment and memories of emotional associations. | Meaning of physical situation expected. Associated memories of such physical situations. |

Resultant arousal level as a combination of environmental factors

Potentially disabling extreme    Tension . . . relaxation continuum    Potentially disabling extreme

Emotional states associated with this level of arousal

Emotion experienced is the one 'known' to be appropriate

his position on the 'tension . . . relaxation' continuum which, in his case, can be assumed to be towards the tension end.

In coming to a decision as to how Mark might best be helped to overcome his problem of head-banging and insufficient sleep, it is now possible to have regard to a whole variety of factors which might be amenable to change. It would, for example, be very easy to come to the concluion that relaxation training will provide the answer. This may well be true, but by adopting such a strategy unquestioningly a whole range of other possible interventions could be disregarded. It is certainly the case that relaxation training will provide Mark with a technique which gives him much greater control over his own responses, but it is equally certain that some of the other aspects of his environment which are outside his control are within the control of his parents. This is an extremely important point which cannot be over-emphasised, and to which reference will be made later. At this point two examples may help to illustrate how beneficial interventions could be made.

Firstly, it would be possible to bring about change in the expected behaviour of the adults to Mark's problem. Having experienced this head-banging over many years from two children, Mark's parents had completely lost patience with their sons and they had only one category of response to the situation. This was to shout up to them in an increasingly irritated fashion telling them to stop, and even at times to resort to physical violence to emphasise their displeasure. Of course they had no expectation at all that these actions would have any effect, but they may have served to relieve their own feelings. There were alternatives open to the parents which they had not thought to investigate. They could have ignored the activity altogether, which might have served to remove some of the anxiety from the situation. They could have adopted a sympathetic approach and provided a soothing presence at bedtime. They could have adopted a 'scientific' approach and timed the length of the episodes in order to institute a programme of reinforcement designed to decrease the time spent head-banging. None of these possibilities was within Mark's control; all of them were within the control of his parents.

Secondly, the parents were in the position to bring about change in the physical environment. It would have been possible to separate the two boys as a bedroom had become vacant. Even without this it would still have been easy to change the layout of the furniture in the room or to redecorate it. These are not actions which would ordinarily seem to be related to the behaviour of Mark and his brother, but there is little doubt that the physical aspects of the environment become significantly associated with arousal level.

Returning to Figure 7.2 it can be seen that the general arousal level present at any specific moment is determined by the contribution of the environmental factors, past, present and future. This general arousal level, in its turn, determines the position on the 'tension . . . relaxation' continuum. It will be recalled that the continuum itself is emotionally neutral and, in fact, nothing that has been described so far as being part of the learning system is experienced at a conscious level. It is best to consider all these processes as taking place physiologically without impinging on our awareness, in much the same way as the heart beats and the lungs breathe and the liver carries out its function. This is not to imply that the awareness of events that have taken place before is not a determining factor regarding the position on the continuum. However, it is the awareness that is current at the time the events are experienced that contributes to the production of a learned physiological response. Such a learned response could conceivably be much more powerful than the response to what is happening currently.

Perhaps this rather complex idea may be better understood by considering a well-known physiological response. If a person is hungry, and various events associated with having a meal are present in the environment, then the likelihoood is that salivation will increase. The sound of a table being prepared for a meal, the sound of activity in the kitchen, as well as the smell of food, can all produce this mouthwatering affect. It is clear that this physiological response can only take place because of learning which is associated with past experiences. The salivation is of itself a neutral event. It is the body's way of making preparation for the intake of food. The memory of what has been experienced before is what induces the salivation, rather than the quality or the flavour of what is to follow or whether the quantity will be sufficient for the body's needs.

When considering the effect of the position currently held on the 'tension . . . relaxation' continuum it can only be significant in the light of the emotional responses with which that position is associated. This leads to a consideration of the learned emotional states and the conscious perception of the state which is appropriate to the current setting. This third aspect of the system must now be considered.


## THE EMOTIONAL RESPONSE

The emotional response comes about as a consequence of the currently held position on the 'tension . . . relaxation' continuum. However, it is not being suggested that there is a simple one-to-one relationship between the emotional response experienced and the arousal level. A particular arousal level may, in fact, be associated with a number of different emotional states. The particular emotional state experienced will be dependent upon the child's previous learning of what is appropriate to the current situation. For example, a high level of arousal could be associated with an emotional response of fear, but equally it could be associated with a feeling of high excitement in anticipation of a greatly desired event. The emotional state experienced will come about because the child has knowledge of the significance of the current environment. This is an important concept because it helps to illustrate the neutrality of the 'tension . . . relaxation' continuum and to emphasise the position taken in this book that emotions are learnt responses. Because this idea is so central to the approach some further illustrations may be helpful.

A commonly reported experience is that of feeling in a 'highly charged' state; of experiencing a feeling of excited anticipation without any recognised associated object for the feeling; of experiencing baseless feelings of fear and dread. Expressions such as 'free-floating anxiety' or 'being on a high' are applied to these curious states. It is as though a position on the 'tension . . . relaxation' continuum is being experienced without any appropriate emotion to which it can be attached. In other words the level of arousal is itself quite neutral, and there is nothing in the current environment which merits the labelling of a particular emotion.

Although the experiences described above will strike a chord with many people, for the majority it will be something which only happens rarely. It is, perhaps, not surprising that the system sometimes comes up with inappropriate signals if due weight is given to the complex nature of the process which produces the arousal level. This is not a problem for most children because of the rarity of its occurrence, but sometimes an example occurs of a child who is at most times anxious or fearful or 'high' for no apparent reason. In such instances relaxation training has been found to be beneficial but it is advisable that it should be carried out under the supervision of a psychologist.

In the vast majority of instances the level of arousal will have come about in response to the child's environmental experiences, and these will have averaged out to produce a position on the 'tension . . . relaxation' continuum. This position will be associated with a number of emotional responses which have been learnt by the child. The particular emotion experienced will be that which is appropriate to the current situation *in the light of the previous experience of the child.*

The appropriateness of the emotion being experienced will be tested against the reality of the current environment, and the emotional response will be strengthened or weakened in the light of this. It is at this point that learning takes place. Figure 7.3 shows how this final link in the chain of events provides not just the current emotional response but a learning experience which feeds back to the bank of knowledge concerning the past.

Returning to the example of Mark, whose behaviour was affected by his lack of sleep and whose ability to get to sleep was in turn affected by his habitual head-banging, it is now possible to complete the account of the strategies adopted to help him. The environmental factors which were under the control of his parents were the first to be dealt with because these could weaken the link between the emotional response and the learning which took place. To achieve this the parents agreed to change their behaviour towards Mark's problems. It was also possible to change the physical environment, and this was done by moving Mark into a different bedroom and separating him from his brother. Attention was then given to those aspects of Mark's personal environment which were equally amenable to change but which were under his own control. He started a course of relaxation training and when he had mastered the technique, which he did very successfully, this was used as a direct means of inducing sleep. He was able to use his relaxation technique as a direct substitution for his head-banging. At last he had an alternative behaviour available to him which could be specifically directed at overcoming his problem. An alternative which was under his own control.

## FROM THEORY TO PRACTICE

Any attempt to provide an explanation of what might be going on in this most complex of organisms is unlikely to be straightforward. Within the person there are the cognitive, the physical and the emotional factors all interacting. Outside the person there are the physical, the social and the temporal aspects of the environment, also busily interacting. Beyond all this is the knowledge of the authors that the interventions they make invariably bring about beneficial changes in unsatisfactory situations. It would be possible to rest our case on this fact alone and to make no attempt to deduce an explanatory model. It would also be possible to concentrate exclusively upon the practical aspects of relaxation training without taking into

**Figure 7.3:** Learning system

| Child's environment | Current situation | | |
|---|---|---|---|
| | Past | Present | Anticipated |
| Personal | Arousal level. Associated emotional states with past arousal level. Genetic endowment, e.g. temperament. | Arousal level. Memory of emotional states at similar times. | Anticipation of what emotions will be felt based upon memories of previously experienced similar situations. |
| Social | Peer group, e.g. classmates, friends. Family, e.g. siblings, parents, extended family. Significant adults, e.g. teachers, neighbours. Behaviour of these towards child. | Significant figures in current situation. Memory of how these behaved previously. | Significant figures expected in future environment and previous experience of them. Expected behaviour of these figures. |
| Physical | Home. School. Neighbourhood. Physical character of these, e.g. colour, sound, smell, furnishings. | Current physical environment. Experiences associated with current physical environment and memories of emotional associations. | Meaning of physical situation expected. Associated memories of such physical situations. |

Resultant arousal level as a combination of environmental factors

↓

Potentially disabling extreme    Tension . . . relaxation continuum    Potentially disabling extreme

↓

Emotional states associated with this level of arousal

↓

Emotion experienced is the one 'known' to be appropriate

consideration the implications of providing young people with this extremely powerful tool. However, to derive the greatest benefit from the approach both the learner, as far as he is able, and the trainer, undoubtedly, should be aware of its power and of its limitations. The following chapter contains some consideration of these matters as a prelude to Chapter 9, where the emphasis is entirely on the practical application of relaxation training.

To conclude this presentation of a model of emotional learning, and before proceeding to the practice of relaxation training, it would be useful to consider the following quotation from Izard and Bueckler (1980).

Emotion activation is mediated by the somatic nervous system, although once an emotion is activated it may arouse autonomic-visceral-glandular activity. This view of emotion activation has important implications for the self-regulation of the emotions, since the somatic nervous system is under voluntary control. For example, if this hypothesis is correct, a person who needed to suppress anger in order to avoid a potentially serious consequence of its expression should be able to attenuate the emotion either by inhibiting the expressive movements of the face and body or *by relaxing the muscles involved* [our italics].

# 8

# Matters Arising

*Certain issues are here given a further airing — for the purposes of developing some ideas, whilst opening the door to some new ones.*

In this chapter a number of points raised in previous chapters are discussed in more detail. These are matters of some significance to the case for relaxation training, and may or may not be contentious. But often we come upon indications of the need for further investigation or research. Some of the questions raised now are open-ended. The reader is invited to consider these issues in the light of his or her own knowledge and experience.

## 1. RELAXATION TRAINING IS *ENABLING*

Relaxation training enables one to think through a situation, to seek and to select from a range of the more constructive kinds of response which might be made to anxiety-provoking situations. So it is worth deliberating on just what are the implications for 'trainee' and 'trainer' — namely, the child and the adult who is responsible for that child. Whilst each child/adult partnershp is different — no two relationships being in every respect the same — there are certain aspects which do seem to be common, and need to be taken into account as the working relationship changes its character.

For instance, there will be a relative shift in control from one party to the other. The adult will find herself relinquishing control just as the child assumes a greater measure of control for his own actions and over his immediate environment. This represents a change of emphasis within the relationship, and with it there is an implicit development in the trust between adult and child. The adult is trusting the child more to get on with helping himself, and the child is encouraged to understand that this is what is happening and to reciprocate that confidence.

At the same time, responsibility tends to pass from the adult to the child. The adult is not so much relinquishing responsibility as actively deciding that the primary responsibility lies with the child. The latter then is less dependent, correspondingly more able to grow in independence.

Such considerations as these bring about a redefinition of the adult's role, and the child's understanding of that role. Clearly, the adult too is faced with the need to accept changes in the child. Particularly for parents, this can prove a testing time, for the child's maturity may appear to put on a spurt and can catch the family unawares. The adult may need to re-emphasise that her caring commitment is no less than before, only changed in character. All in all, a few readjustments become necessary — and that's usually no bad thing!

There are also implications, more subtle perhaps, which concern the principal environments governing our behaviour — depicted in an earlier chapter as the physical, the social and the personal.

Given that the desired end-product is a child who is more relaxed, less anxious and more able to cope, then some degree of deliberate, active relaxation of the physical surroundings is an obvious initial step to take. Moreover, it is an inevitable outcome once relaxation training has been undertaken and applied. The presence of soft, comfortable and familiar furnishings, the absence of any hazards, irritants and obstacles, and the explicit clarification of what is wanted or is appropriate at any given time . . . all serve to relax the atmosphere, to make things easy and to allow what is wanted to actually happen.

Similarly, the social environment needs to take cognisance of the fact that a child 'enabled' is a child more active, more prepared, more willing and more able to exert a positive influence over his environment. Overtures to the child can be made more confidently, they will more often be returned, and frequently they will in fact be initiated by the child who is now more comfortable in the social setting. If a particular person or people in general have been a source of concern to the child in the past, and are less so in the present, then a mutual coming-to-terms is under way.

For the child — for anyone — at a personal level the implications can be almost limitless. Relaxation training can enable so much, but even in its context simply as an educational aid, doors open and opportunities beckon as perhaps never before. Personal communications and relationships are more likely to be enhanced and broadened. On the other hand, each individual has to discover his own limitations, and find out what being less dependent, for example, means in day-to-day terms. The limitations, too, of any relaxation technique, like anything else, vary from one individual to another and some people will be more enabled than others, just as some situations will prove more responsive than others.

It is not unrealistic then to ask whether the 'world-out-there' is ready for, say, troubled or deviant or severely handicapped persons of whatever age, who have become more able to exert greater control over their own lives, thereby influencing everyone else's too. In our own culture, segregation is giving way to some degree of social integration of those individuals and groups hitherto on the fringe at best. This signals the need to create, for example, more ramps in supermarkets, etc., to allow wheelchair access, more life-space generally, increased opportunities in the job market, more everything for people previously restricted and denied. Society creates the expectation that we all can help best by helping others help themselves.

Returning finally and more specifically to the world of children, and those in care of children, could it be that adult needs, values and priorities are often served by maintaining the younger generation's dependence on adults' greater experience and conformity? The enabling aspect of the adult/child relationship implies negotiation and compromise, a contractual agreement to seek the same or similar ends. If the caring adult, however, feels unable or unwilling to *enable* the child, then perhaps the adult is putting her needs before those of the child.

## 2. TO WHAT EXTENT IS *UNDER-AROUSAL* A PROBLEM?

Whilst we have been predominantly concerned with the difficulties associated with excess tension, usually known as anxiety, or identified in certain forms of chronic motor impairment, it is accepted that some degree of tension is necessary for constructive action. Sometimes what is lacking is a level of preparedness for the undertaking of a task. To the extent that this raises the whole subject of motivation it is beyond the scope of the present discussion. But lack of motivation may sometimes be characterised as under-arousal or too low a level of muscular tension for any kind of satisfactory participation in necessary activity.

Now, under-arousal may refer to 'too low an arousal level' — that is, a temperamental state or personality characteristic dominating one's attitude such that one is rarely sufficiently aroused to do anything. But even accepting that we all have different thresholds of arousal, relaxation training still offers a useful array of skills, since we all need to relax or to tense as circumstances dictate. The relaxation exercises described in the first chapter of this book argue for the need to tense the various muscle groups first, in order to experience the difference between feeling tense and feeling relaxed. It is the ready and immediate recognition of unhelpful tensions that triggers off the relaxation response.

The more usual state of affairs, however, is not that we are either permanently disposed to be under-aroused or to be over-aroused, but that we experience feelings of relaxation *and* feelings of anxiety to varying degrees most days of the week. Under-arousal then refers to a point or possibly a stage on the 'tension . . . relaxation' continuum — a much more dynamic concept — and, as such, represents behaviour more amenable to change. Since the world in which we live does tend to project tensions, how then do we cope, if we have been successful in creating in our immediate environment circumstances which are conducive to relaxation? The answer must be that we need to develop the art of tensing sufficiently when necessary! Otherwise, and more realistically, relaxation training is a matter of learning to relax to enable the handling of tension.

Arguably it is possible to teach someone or oneself to develop the relaxation response to the degree where a relaxed state becomes the norm, and more than that, where an abnormally relaxed state becomes that person's norm! In such a situation, presumably the person never bothers about anything! This has to be a hypothetical situation unless no action is ever necessary in that person's lifestyle. But we all need to be active to some extent, and to that extent we need tensions too. What we do not need is anxiety which cripples and prevents constructive action of any kind. Neither do we need under-arousal and we combat its influence by learning to tense when necessary.

Clearly there are many ways of creating necessary tension — a pacy lifestyle or a sporting outlet fits the bill. The need to create tension is quite explicit in the language and experience of us all as we deal with under-arousal. The latter may be perceived as low motivation or depression or lethargy — or any such term which conjures up an image of precious little action! And what sort of solution is advocated? To 'get up and go' . . . to 'give oneself a good shake!' . . . to 'stir yourself' . . . or 'pull yourself together!'. The tired business-woman, returning home in the evening to cook a family meal and later to catch up on the housework, will manage everything if her low motivation in fact triggers off muscular activity. The long-distance runner keeps finding more miles in road-weary legs, because each twinge of under-arousal stimulates just enough tension to overcome fatigue.

The simple message when it comes to dealing with under-arousal is: do something! Bearing in mind too that the body's reaction to tension is to follow it with relaxation, then this message is worth heeding. If under-arousal does take the form of something which inhibits the get-up-and-go approach, as in the case of chronic depression or when one is absorbed with fear, how salutary then to have available an habitual response — that of tensing or relaxing to order. Daily doses of relaxation training do help establish such a pattern of reaction, so that if for whatever reason 'doing something' — that is, taking a physical outlet — is not possible, concentration on creating tension (paradoxically) through relaxation training will provide the required uplift.

## 3. DESENSITISATION

Reference was made in Chapter 5, 'De-fusing Anxiety', to the therapeutic practice known as 'desensitisation'. This technique is not always the most apposite way to handle the management of anxiety. Another method, known as 'flooding', is a technique which suffuses the subject with the anxiety-provoking stimulus and so puts the lower-order anxiety into more manageable perspective — the subject, having been to hell and back, is now more relaxed in facing relatively minor anxiety-provoking situations. Similarly, other effective techniques enable the subject to tackle the anxiety-provoking stimulus in a more relaxed fashion.

The relevant literature is undecided as to the merits of one technique over another, but, so far as children are concerned, flooding too often presents an unmanageable element of risk. The child may be required to face quite overwhelming threats with which he has no strategy to deal, even in his imagination let alone in real life. His parents or caring adults may find themselves faced with a corresponding escalation of anxiety which they too cannot handle. A desensitisation approach, on the other hand, which 'desensitises' all parties to any imminent or actual anxiety, is the kinder and indeed the more effective route to follow. It eliminates one anxiety at a time, *teaching* a strategy as it goes along. The younger, quicker learner is thus at an advantage.

So far as other techniques are concerned, whether the approach is predominantly behavioural or psychodynamic, of prime importance is the requirement to foster a relaxed and purposeful relationship between therapist and client, between adult and child. Without the establishment of such a bond, no therapy will work. To underline this assertion, Truax and Carkhuff were maintaining as long ago as 1967 that any successful counselling approach and intervention relies on foundations of empathy and understanding, and an accurate assessment of 'the problem'.

Much has already been made of the idea of relaxation as an enabling skill or strategy, which intervenes between facing the anxiety and arriving at a constructive solution. Whether or not anxiety does present itself as a dominant factor initially, the relaxation response — having already been learned — intervenes, enables and makes the learning of alternative responses (new skills) more probable. Alternatively, new responses may well be learned, and taught, as direct alternatives to the present 'problem' behaviour. In such cases, anxiety is not an issue, intervening relaxation skills are probably unnecessary, so desensitisation will achieve less than a more 'direct' form of behaviour therapy.

## 4. THE THREE-COLUMN *HIERARCHY* MODEL

Let us pursue the subject of what to do about anxiety once it has been recognised, by looking further into the notion of the 'anxiety hierarchy'. Building a hierarchy of anxieties, in order to consider and tackle them in a meaningful order, is seen as a valuable aspect of behavioural counselling itself. A compact discussion of the subject more appropriately referred to as 'systematic desensitisation' is given in Nelson-Jones' fuller text on 'counselling psychology' (1982).

The use of a three-column hierarchy in particular, to effect desensitisation, helps adult and child alike to find a constructive solution to anxiety. It is also a way of assessing in a relatively straightforward and objective manner whether the anxieties felt are amenable to desensitisation at all, and whether indeed it is anxiety that is the priority to be dealt with.

In representing a person's fears, or traumatic events, or moments of excruciating horror, etc. on any credible model — then that person is at once distanced from what has been so worrying him and something like realism returns. Seeing matters in terms of the three-column hierarchy, of 'the situation', 'the response', and 'the outcome' — this form of perception is itself a strategy. But it is essentially a strategy for dealing with anxiety by teaching/learning to respond in a more relaxed fashion. The model is not so useful if anxiety is not a dominant factor.

As has been suggested earlier, anxiety, like relaxation, can be interpreted as an intervening response. If anxiety is not a significant factor and thus a problem itself, but if a different final response or end-result is wanted, then a new behaviour may be taught and learned, one which is incompatible with the old. Thus, a more direct form of intervention or therapy can be more serviceable. Direct intervention, along the lines of 'behaviour modification', would usually deal at once with the most troublesome behaviour — whereas the approach of anxiety management through desensitisation is always to tackle the least anxious situation first.

The three columns, moreover , noticeably correspond to 'the past', 'the present' and 'the anticipated' of the learning system described in Chapter 7 — and so make sense to the different parties trying to find solutions to anxiety-laden problems. There is an obvious advantage in trying to do something about the setting conditions and the immediate past, in an effort to prevent anxiety taking root. This too implies an objective evaluation of the situation. For all concerned, perhaps the most profitable line of endeavour is to try to strike a balance between taking adequate account of the past experience and circumstances of one's life, and actually coping with the situation as one finds it. The arguments in favour of having accessible some form of battle plan, conceived and tested in advance, are unequivocal. This particular model — the three-column anxiety hierarchy which encourages desensitisation — requires some refinement yet, but does have a great deal to offer.

## 5. THE CUE

Earlier chapters have spoken of a continuum, 'tension . . . relaxation', and in the present chapter (section 3 above) reference was made to relaxation as an intervening skill. Logically, then, there is a range of intervening responses possible, of which anxiety and deep relaxation are the extremes. So we can think of an intervening response as one which somehow is triggered or introduced into the sequence of available responses. Relaxation is an intervening response which has been introduced into the sequence, not merely of available, but of appropriate, responses. Relaxation and anxiety being mutually incompatible, one or the other dominates as the intervening response. Some device, hereafter known as the 'cue', can facilitate the triggering of the relaxation response.

For our purposes then, the cue is a stimulus (an event, a word, an idea, etc.) which is learned to be associated with relaxation. The association can be taught, at a conscious or subliminal level (e.g.

through hypnosis). The cue may be self-induced or prompted by a trusted 'outsider'.

It represents a link in a chain of preparatory behaviours. The 'image', which was introduced in Chapter 1, is the cue to relax a given muscle group. As such it is the last (before actual relaxation takes place) in the chain of preparatory behaviours. The other links include getting the room ready, setting the cassette tape, etc. There is an identifiable sequence: first comes the range of preparation, then the cue, followed by the relaxation response.

A similar idea is employed by Sharpe and Lewis in their *Fight your phobia* . . . . They advocate 'cue cards', as used by television newsreaders for instance, to help disrupt any rising anxiety, by periodically inducing trusted cues to restore calm.

The significance of the cue should not be under-estimated. For some people an increase in tension sounds a more or less immediate warning, and they respond with relaxation of the muscles: in these cases, the tension *is* the cue. For most people, perhaps for everyone most of the time, there is some degree of latency of response when relaxation is delayed: what stimulates the relaxed response eventually is a cue which has been previously experienced and found effective.

That an intervening response may be introduced through a cue — that is, stimulated by 'something hitherto unrelated' — fits nicely into a classical conditioning model. Anderson and Ausubel (1965) provide one of the more comprehensive and comprehensible accounts of how different forms of conditioning operate. Certainly the concept of the 'intervening response' has occupied behaviour theorists for many years now. Note that a cue may equally induce anxiety or relaxation (or whatever). So when we talk of intervening to offset anxiety, we need a very powerful and reliable relaxation cue indeed, and the technique must serve to put the subject very much in control.

The following paradigm represents four discrete stages in learning. Even if it is conceptually over-simplified, it does describe clearly the development of a response or response set, characterised by relaxation on the one hand, anxiety on the other.

| (key: | CS | .... conditioned stimulus |
|---|---|---|
| | UCS | .... unconditioned stimulus |
| | CR | .... conditioned response |
| | UCR | .... unconditioned response |
| | rel | .... relaxation |
| | anx | .... anxiety |
| | situ | .... potentially anxiety-provoking situation) |

|  | RELAXED RESPONSE | ANXIOUS RESPONSE |
|---|---|---|
| stage1. | CScue.> CRrel | CScue.>CRanx |
| stage2. | UCSsitu.>(CScue.>CRrel) .>UCRrel.>+ve. outcome | UCSsitu.>(CScue.>CRanx) .>UCRanx.>panic |
| stage3. | UCSsitu.>CRrel .>UCRrel.>faster, positive outcome | UCSsitu.>CRanx .>UCRanx.>escalating anxiety |
| stage4. | UCSsitu.>UCRrel .>consistently +ve. | UCSsitu.>UCRanx .>habitual panic |

In such a model there is no impediment to learning a relaxed response at least as capably as learning to become anxious! Stage 1 is the initial training procedure; stage 2 shows how whenever an anxiety-provoking situation arises, the previous learning link is called up; by stage 3 the cue becomes redundant; and at stage 4 there is greater immediacy of response.

The 14-year-old Paul, to whom reference was made in Chapter 5, was taught how to achieve relaxation in the psychologist's counselling room, then reinforced his relaxed (conditioned) response in the quiet of his own home (stage 1). On returning home even a little late of an evening he would feel anxious, so he learned to apply his relaxation skills to help bring his worry under control (stage 2). In due course he became able to contemplate his returning home at whatever hour in a relaxed manner (stage 3). Eventually coming home in the evening held no anxieties for the youth, he could be quite rational about it and his time-keeping actually improved (stage 4).

## 6. IMPLICATIONS OF THE *CEREBRAL PALSY* STUDIES

In Chapter 6 relaxation training was being explored and then advocated as an educational aid. Its enabling potential for severely handicapped CP children was one of several related aspects which were discussed. Some of the follow-up work with different CP children is now briefly described as being of particular relevance to the subject of relaxation training.

One project has taken the form of an experiment in trying to relax profoundly, multiple-handicapped CP young children, and creating conditions helpful to relaxation so that the children might relax as needed away from their training location.

Three boys and three girls, average age seven years, were each in turn given an 'a–b–a' experimental training programme. This consisted of a baseline task — 'solving' a computer maze by means of sensor pads — (a); there then followed a period of relaxation training undertaken at home in some instances, and in all cases at school taught by educational psychologists — (b); finally after no training at all in the maze game the baseline task was again presented — (c).

The relaxation training was as near as possible a standardised procedure for all the children; but some parents helped their child further at home, while others did not. From the first encounter with the computerised maze until the second and last, just three months elapsed, three weeks of which were 'lost' in school holidays.

Each child learned, and as others had done previously learned quickly, the basic skill of relaxing to instruction. To the verbal cue 'relax', each was able to release muscular tension, and in time could generalise this ability to relax anywhere within the school grounds — certainly, anyway, if not put under any pressure.

Apart from the cue, the setting conditions preparatory to relaxation included an element of personal and physical contact. Otherwise the training and, up to a point, the application followed the same conditioning model as described above.

These children gave inconclusive evidence only, of an ability to *use* their relaxation skill when confronting the maze task the second time of asking. One of the six was relaxed enough to try different methods of approach to the problem of the maze — in itself no mean achievement. All of the children showed some improvement at their second maze attempt, but the measure of improvement was not statistically significant — a churlish observation perhaps! What *is* significant, however, is that relaxation training is one effective means of helping severely disabled children to relax, and offers hope where previously there was very little.

As has been indicated before, the CP studies involve a great many variables, and one imponderable, namely the sheer awesomeness of the condition in its more extreme forms. Again, though, there is good reason to explore further the potential of relaxation, as an aid to all manner of learning and as a means whereby children and young people are enabled to act much more usefully on their own behalf.

# 9

## Teaching How to Relax

*Teaching relaxation techniques should not be undertaken without a full appreciation of what is involved. Learning the technique yourself, and reading the preceding chapters, will have prepared you for this sensitive enterprise. A step-by-step guide follows, accompanied by a suggested protocol.*

Is relaxation training necessary? This may seem a somewhat perverse question to pose in a book which is devoted to the promotion of relaxation training, but perhaps it will sound a necessary note of caution. Such a cautionary note is required for a number of reasons, not the least of which is to prevent parents or others in care of children from rushing in with what they may regard as a universal panacea for all emotional problems. It is also important to realise that relaxation training should not be embarked upon as something which can be done to children without enlisting their cooperation and their commitment, because the whole thrust of the approach is that of enabling children to gain control. Another reason for applying caution before embarking on relaxation training is the need to give due weight to the environment in which the anxiety-directed behaviour is taking place.

This chapter of the book is directed towards providing a practical step-by-step guide to relaxation training as a means of helping children to cope with anxiety. Part of the process is to look as carefully as possible at the total 'life space' in which the child's behaviour is situated. It may sometimes become clear, as a result of this investigation, that relaxation training is not an appropriate means to employ to alleviate the anxiety, or at the very least that it needs to be accompanied by other strategies. It is important also for adults who propose to utilise these techniques to become familiar with the consequences of the training. In fact, it is doubtful whether those who have not themselves attained mastery of relaxation training would be effective in teaching it to others. Finally, it must be stressed that relaxation training is not something which can be universally applied like a remedy bought across the counter in a chemist's shop. The individual person who is to receive the training and the specific nature of the problems which are being displayed must all be taken into account.

114

All these aspects are dealt with in the following guide, and it cannot be emphasised too strongly that intending trainers of relaxation techniques should make themselves familiar with all the steps involved before training is commenced.

## THE SETTING FOR ANXIETY

A common failing amongst many adults who are concerned with children and their problems is that they focus solely on the problem itself to the exclusion of the setting in which it is taking place. Considerable attention has been paid to this setting in making the case for relaxation training throughout this book. It has been referred to as the child's physical, social and personal environment. Its dynamic nature has been emphasised by looking at these aspects of the environment in the past, in the present and in the future. Much of the discussion in previous chapters has been directed towards showing how these various environmental factors are involved in determining the currently held position on the 'tension . . . relaxation' continuum. Although the position on this continuum may be altered by employing the techniques of relaxation it may also be altered by changes in the environmental factors themselves. Sometimes such changes may be brought about by the actions of the adults within the child's personal environment. Sometimes they may be brought about by the child himself when he is made aware of their amenability for change. Frequently, a combination of relaxation training and changes brought about in the environment will be rewarded with the greatest success.

In this preliminary stage, before any decision is made as to whether relaxation training should be undertaken, it is best to adopt a logical sequence of steps designed to gather as much information as possible about the problem itself and the setting in which it occurs.

## Step 1

*The problem*

1.  Define the problem, e.g. you can use the anxiety hierarchy outlined in Chapter 5.
2.  Who perceives the problem? The parents? The teachers? The child?
3.  What is its exact nature? Is it related to anxiety?
4.  How does the child experience the anxiety? Fear? Anger? Dread?

115

Worry? Running away? Clinging to adults? Vague illnesses? Feeling sick?

## Step 2

*The physical environment*

1. Where, in the past, has the anxiety-related behaviour occurred?
2. Is the current physical environment the same as that which obtained in the past?
3. Is the future physical environment in which the anxiety-related behaviour can be expected to recur likely to be the same as it has been in the past?
4. Is it possible for the child, or more likely the adults responsible for him, to bring about significant changes in the physical environment?

## Step 3

*The social environment*

1. Who are the significant adults in the child's social environment? These will include parents, relations, teachers, etc. Their effect upon the child might be positive or negative or a combination of both.
2. Is it possible to relate the anxious behaviour displayed by the child with actions engaged in by these adults?
3. If adult behaviour appears to be related to the anxious behaviour of the child is it possible to persuade them (or yourself) to modify their actions?
4. Try to put yourself in the place of the child and ask the question, 'Have I good reason to be worried about this?'

## Step 4

*The personal environment*

1. Does the child perceive that he has a problem?
2. If the child is aware of having a problem does he wish to bring about change?
3. If he does not understand that change in his behaviour would improve his situation is it possible that he would understand if

this was to be explained to him?

4. Is he able to follow the relaxation training instructions?
5. Would he be able to use the technique unaided once taught, or would he require an adult to cue him into using it?

## Step 5

1. Consider all the information that you have collected by asking the questions contained in the previous four steps.
2. In the light of this information is relaxation training indicated as a means of alleviating the problem, or would some other method be more appropriate, e.g. behaviour modification?
3. Should the relaxation training be accompanied by environmental changes engineered by the adults?

## Step 6

1. Before attempting to use relaxation training with a child, undertake the training yourself by using the programme outlined in Chapter 1.

## Step 7

1. Decide on the approach to be adopted for teaching the relaxation technique.

You can use the methods outlined in this chapter, adapting the scripts to suit the individual child. If you have carried out the training yourself you will probably wish to employ some of the ideas developed in Chapter 1.

## RELAXATION — TEACHING THE TECHNIQUE

It is not suggested that there is only one method of learning the technique of relaxation. The authors each use more than one, and they do not both use precisely the same selection of methods. There exist very good reasons for these variations. The individual differences between children have been emphasised on many occasions throughout the text, and some of the variations in approach are intended to accommodate to these differences. For example, it would have been completely inappropriate to use the same methodology and the same language for Joanne, our very bright, anorexic teenager, and Richard, the little boy attending a special school. Clearly, too, our little spastic children, some of whom had no expressive language, required an approach designed for their individual needs.

Part of the skill of using relaxation techniques is the ability to recognise which training method is likely to be successful for a particular child or for a particular problem which is being experienced. It is sometimes quite important to personalise the tape being used by introducing the name of the child at a few points. Sometimes it is necessary, during the latter stages of the training, to make specific reference to the problem which the child is experiencing. A good example of this is when the aim is to help a child to overcome a stammer. With such difficulties it is often useful to agree with the child a cue that may be used to induce relaxation as he approaches words which he knows cause him to stammer. This approach was used with a first-year university student who was studying Russian. Perhaps one might reasonably question the wisdom of choosing such a subject, which entailed a great deal of oral work, by a young man who had stammered since he was a child. However, it was his interest and, apart from his stammer, he excelled at the subject. By teaching him the techniques of relaxation, and by carefully analysing his speech in order to identify those sounds which could be guaranteed to induce his stammer, it became possible for him to use a cue which prepared him for the approaching difficulty. Within a few weeks he was tackling his oral work with greatly increased confidence and he finally took a good degree.

The remainder of this chapter will be devoted to giving a detailed account of one relaxation training approach. Actual texts are given which may be adapted for individual children. In most instances it is recommended that the instructions should be recorded. There are a number of reasons for this preference. The aim is to give the child a technique which he is able to use independently, and it is therefore important that the amount of support he receives during the training sessions is kept to a minimum. By operating in this way the relationship becomes that between a depersonalised voice and himself. As the training proceeds the importance of the voice decreases whilst the importance of the message which it carries increases in significance.

The next decision to be made is concerned with whose voice should be on the recording. It is important that the voice should be soothing and clear, and there would also be some merit in the voice having a minimum of associations with a person well known to the child. For this reason, parents may not always be the best people to take on this task. Persuade someone with a suitable voice from outside the regular contacts which the child has to do the job for you. Of course, it is for you to select, to modify and to supply the text that is to be used.

A further advantage of using recorded instructions is that the child can get on with the training without having to rely on somebody else finding the time to spend with him. Finally, the tape recording can always be relied upon to use exactly the same words on each occasion, and this consistency is highly desirable.

## RELAXATION TRAINING

This method, which has been employed successfully on numerous occasions, consists of five phases, three of which comprise the personal contributions of the therapist whilst the other two phases are presented by means of tape recordings.

### Phase 1: Introduction

This consists of an interview with the child, during which his problems are discussed. The main purpose of this interview is two-fold. It is first of all necessary to determine whether the problem being experienced is rooted in anxiety, tension or some other form of uncontrolled emotional response. At this interview some consideration would be given to the antecedents of the problem and to the consequences which follow upon the emotional behaviour produced. This aspect of the interview is covered in Chapter 5. The second major purpose of this interview is to discover whether the child himself sees that he has a problem — the likelihood is extremely strong that it will have been brought to the attention of the therapist by someone other than the child. If he does recognise that he has a problem it is important to determine if he wishes to do anything about it. A useful concept to bear in mind is that behaviour is only repeated if it is reinforced, i.e. some reward is associated with its production. 'Problem' behaviour perceived by an adult may serve some function for the child. For example, temper tantrums may result in his getting his own way or in gaining attention and comfort. Joanne's anorexia placed her in a position of power and control. Richard's inappropriate shouting caused him to be removed from situations which he found threatening. However, these rewarding consequences are often followed by feelings of remorse, shame or regret, and in most instances children recognise that there is greater satisfaction to be gained from a cessation of a behaviour which is caused by being out of control emotionally. It is this aspect of gaining control over the emotions — the ability to prevent a loss of temper, to overcome feelings of fear, to halt rising panic — which persuades most children that they would like to embark upon a course of training to achieve this end.

## Phase 2

Having obtained the agreement of the child that relaxation training should go ahead a second interview is arranged. At this interview the therapist provides an explanation of the rationale which underpins such training. The level of explanation will depend upon the age and the ability of the child. With some children a reasonably detailed explanation of the relationship between arousal and efficiency may be given; with others the discussion may deal with those 'funny feelings which you get in your tummy'. In all cases the reason for the use of the training to be undertaken is explained because at no time is the child seen to be a passive recipient of a therapy being imposed by someone outside himself.

If a biofeedback instrument is to be used it is introduced at this stage. In order to ensure that the child is not made anxious by the instrument the usual ploy is for the therapist to connect the electrodes to himself to start with, and to carry out a demonstration of its function. The child is then invited to try it himself. To date this ploy has never failed! However, it cannot be emphasised too often that biofeedback instruments are not necessary for the successful application of relaxation training, and that they are probably better left to be used by professional therapists.

At this second interview the child is presented with the cassette containing Phase 3 of the training programme.

## Phase 3

This phase consists of the first of two recorded relaxation training programmes. It is designed to help the child to appreciate the feeling of relaxation, and this is done by contrasting it with feelings of muscular tension. A full text is given to assist readers to make their own tapes, but it should be borne in mind that this needs to be adapted according to the level of understanding of the individual child. Spaces are left in the text at points where it is considered suitable for the insertion of the child's name. The child is told that he should lie down on his bed to listen to the tape. He is also told how often he should listen to the tape. Usually it is suggested that Tape 1 should be used once a day for a week before proceeding to Tape 2. At this interview an arrangement is made for the next meeting with the therapist. This will usually take place two weeks after the commencement of the training so that the child will have completed Tape 1 and started Tape 2.

*Tape 1* (spaces '— — — — —' are left in which to insert the child's name).

Lie down on your bed. Lie very still. Now close your eyes. — — — — — I want you to take a deep breath. (Pause) Good. Now let it go. Take another deep breath. Let it go slowly. Another deep breath. Slowly let it go. Good.

Now I want you to clench one of your fists. Clench it hard — now let it go. Clench it again — hard — now let it go. Clench the other fist — let it go. Clench it again — let it go — relax. Good

Now I want you to screw up the toes of one foot — tense them hard — good — now let them go — relax. Screw up the toes of your other foot — tense them hard — now let them go — relax.

See if you can clench both fists together — tense them — let them go — relax.

See if you can screw up all your toes — tense them — relax.

Now tense your fists and your feet all together — tense them — good — hold them tense — now let them go — relax.

— — — — — you are learning how to make your muscles go hard — to tense them. And you are learning how to let them go — to relax them. Remember these words — — — — —. Tense — makes your muscles go hard. Relax — makes your muscles let go. I want you to do this with some other muscles.

(At this point the following list of parts of the body should be inserted one by one in the order given into the spaces '. . . . .' in the text.)

Leg, arm, bottom, shoulders, neck, face, all your body together.

Tense the muscles of one . . . . . Hold them tense. Let them go — relax.

Tense the muscles of one . . . . . again. Let them go — relax.

Tense the muscles of the other . . . . . Hold them tense. Let them go — relax.

Tense the muscles of the other . . . . . again. Let them go — relax. Very good.

That's very good — — — — —.

Take a deep breath — hold it — let it go. Another deep breath — hold it — let it go.

Lie still for a few moments and get up when you are ready.


## Phase 4: Tape 2

Now — — — — — you know how to tense different parts of your body and how to let them go — to relax them. Remember, relax means to let your muscles go slack — relax means to let your muscles go limp and floppy.

The next part of this tape will teach you how to relax your body. It takes quite a long time to learn how to relax really well. I want you to listen to this tape every day until I come back to see you again. You must listen very carefully and do exactly what the tape says.

— — — — — I am going to teach you how to relax. Lie down on your bed. Put your arms by your side and put your legs out straight. Now close your eyes.

* First of all I want you to take a deep breath — hold it — now let it go. Take two more deep breaths in your own time. Hold them and let them go slowly. (Pause to give time for this to be done.) That's good.

Now I want you to think about your feet. Let your feet relax — let them go — let them feel very heavy and very relaxed. Now let that heavy feeling go up your legs until it reaches your knees. Feel the heavy relaxed feeling climb up your legs from your feet up to your knees.

Now let the heavy, relaxed feeling go over your knees into your thighs. Both your legs now feel very heavy, very relaxed and very comfortable — good.

Let this heavy feeling climb higher up your body into your tummy. Let the muscles in your tummy become very heavy, very relaxed and very comfortable. Now let the heavy feeling go up into your chest making your chest feel very heavy, very relaxed — good.

— — — — —, think about your hands. Let them go very floppy, very heavy, very relaxed. Now let the heavy feeling climb all the way up your arms so that they feel very comfortable, very relaxed. Now let your shoulders relax, let them become very heavy and very comfortable. Let your neck muscles relax — let them become very heavy, very comfortable. And now let all the muscles of your face relax. All your body is now relaxed, very heavy, very comfortable and very still. *

Now — — — — —, I want you to go through all these relaxation exercises again. Are you ready? (At this point you should repeat all the text contained between the asterisks.)

Just breathe deeply a few times. Enjoy the feeling of heaviness, of relaxation. That's good. When you are ready you can get up from your bed.

## Phase 5

By the time this phase is reached the child will have mastered the technique of relaxation. This mastery is usually attained after some two weeks of listening to Tape 2. If a biofeedback instrument is available it can be used at this point to demonstrate to the child his newly won ability to bring about relaxation. However, the cue for relaxation to take place is still the sound of the voice on the tape. The next important step is to substitute a self-operated cue. The form that this will take will depend upon the individual child and, where it is possible to do so, this should be decided by discussion and by using your knowledge of the child. For some children the deep breathing which takes place at frequent intervals during the training will provide an effective cue. For others it has been found successful to help them search their memories to recall particularly peaceful and relaxed scenes from their holdiays. Water slowly flowing under a bridge in the quiet of the countryside, lying on the beach on a hot summer's day with only the sound of the waves breaking are typical examples. Anything which is evocative of peacefulness and of comfort and tranquillity will provide a suitable cue.

Tape 2 is used again to help the child internalise the cue which will serve as a 'trigger' for relaxation. He is told to listen to the tape again but this time to sit in a chair and to bring his cue to mind every time he is told to breathe deeply. If he is not to have an imagined scene for his cue then it is usually suggested that he should count very slowly to himself during the time it takes to inhale and exhale.

A further week of this training is usually sufficient. All that then remains is to have a further discussion with the child and to demonstrate that by using his cue he is able to bring about relaxation without having to rely on external help. A biofeedback instrument will show this very clearly, but if one is not available the child himself will report his own feeling of relaxation and the therapist will be able to observe the relaxed bodily attitude. The face and the hands tend to show this very clearly.

From this point it is only a matter of discussing with the child how he is now able to 'trigger' his relaxation at those times when he is aware of a rising feeling of anxiety, panic, fear, loss of temper or whatever it is that has caused him problems.

Sometimes it is necessary, with younger or less able children, for the adult to remind the child to relax at the appropriate time. In such instances the word 'relax' has always been found to be effective.

In conclusion, it is important to emphasise again that the technique of relaxation is one which is intended to place the child 'in control'. This being the case it is for the child himself to decide whether or not to use the technique. Many children find that their newly won ability to keep their anxieties in check has all kinds of positive consequences. Friendless children find friends, fearful children acquire confidence, quick-tempered children gain tranquillity. For some it represents the first step towards an independence of action that will help them to go forward into an adulthood where they are equipped better than most to cope with 'the slings and arrows of outrageous fortune'.

# Bibliography

Anderson, R.C. and Ausubel, D.P. (eds) (1965) *Readings in the psychology of cognition*, Holt, Rinehart & Winston, New York
Bandura, A. (1977) *Social learning theory*, Prentice-Hall, Englewood Cliffs, New Jersey
—— and Walters, R.H. (1964) *Social learning and personality development*, Holt, Rinehart & Winston, New York
Bernstein, D.A. and Borkovec, T.D. (1973) *Progressive relaxation training: a manual for the helping professions*, Research Press, Illinois
Blackham, G.J. and Silberman, A. (1975) *Modification of child and adolescent behaviour*, Wadsworth Press, California
Burch, D.B. and Kanter, D.R. (1984) Individual differences. In Warne, J.S. (ed.), *Sustained attention in human performance*, John Wiley & Sons, New York and Chichester
Cheesman, P.L. and Watts, P. (1985) *Positive behaviour management*. Croom Helm, London/Nichols, New York
Cooper, C.I. (1983) *Stress research*. John Wiley & Sons, New York and Chichester
Davies, D.R. and Tune, G.F. (1970) *Human vigilance performance*, Staples Press, London
Donaldson, M., Grieve, R. and Pratt, C. (1983) *Early childhood development and education*, Blackwell Scientific Publications, Oxford and Boston
Dryden, W. and Golden, W. (1986) *Cognitive behavioural approaches to psychotherapy*, Harper & Row, London and New York
Finnie, N. (1968) *Handling the young cerebral palsied child at home*, William Heinemann, London
Gillham, W. (ed.) (1978) *Reconstructing educational psychology*, Croom Helm, London
Gray, J.A. (1982) *The neuropsychology of anxiety*, Oxford University Press, Oxford and New York
Grossman, S.B. (1967) *A textbook of physiological psychology*, John Wiley & Sons, New York.
Hammersley, M. and Woods, P. (1976) *The process of schooling*, Routledge & Kegan Paul, London and New York
Harrison, A. (1975) Studies of neuromuscular control in normal and spastic individuals. In Holt, K. (ed.), *Movement and child development*, Spastics International Medical Publications, London
Herbert, M. (1978) *Conduct disorders of childhood and adolescence*, John Wiley & Sons, New York and Chichester
Hersen, M. and Bellack, A. (eds) (1976) *Behavioural assessment*, Pergamon Press, New York and Oxford
Hurlock, E.B. (1974) *Personality development*, McGraw-Hill, New York
Izard, C.E. (1972) *The face of emotion*, Appleton-Century Crofts, New York
—— and Bueckler, S. (1980) Aspects of consciousness and personality in terms of differential emotions theory. In Plutchik, R. and Kellerman, H. (eds),

*Emotion: theory, research and experience*, Academic Press, New York and London

Jacobsen, E. (1938) *Progressive relaxation*, University of Chicago Press, Chicago

Leitenberg, H. (ed.) (1976) *Handbook of behaviour modification and behaviour therapy*, Prentice-Hall, Englewood Cliffs, New Jersey

Mackworth, J.F. (1970) *Vigilance and attention: a signal detection approach*, Penguin Books, Harmondsworth

Madders, J. (1973) *Relax*, BBC Publications, London

Mandler, G. (1976) *Mind and emotion*. John Wiley & Sons, New York and Chichester

—— (1980) The generation of emotion: a psychological theory. In Plutchik, R. and Kellerman, H. (eds), *Emotion: theory, research and experience*, Academic Press, New York and London

Marcer, D. (1986) *Biofeedback and related therapies in clinical practice*, Croom Helm, London/Aspen Publishers, Rockville, Maryland

Musson, P.H., Conger, J.J. and Kagan, J. (1963) *Child development and personality*, Harper & Row, London and New York

Nelson-Jones, R. (1982) *The theory and practice of counselling psychology*, Holt, Rinehart & Winston, New York

Piaget, J. (1929) *The child's conception of the world*, Routledge & Kegan Paul, London

—— and Inhelder, B. (1969) *The psychology of the child*, Routledge & Kegan Paul, London and New York

Poteet, J.A. (1973) *Behaviour modification*, Hodder & Stoughton, Sevenoaks

Reisenzein, R. (1983) The Schachter theory of emotion: two decades later, *Psychological Bulletin*, 94 (2) (Sept.) 239–264

Russell, P. (1979) *The brain book*, Routledge & Kegan Paul, London and New York

Schachter, S. (1965) The interaction of cognitive and physiological determinants of emotional state. In Liederman, P.H. and Shapiro, D. (eds) *Psychobiological approaches to social behaviour*, Tavistock Publications, London and New York

Sharpe, R. and Lewis, D. (1979) *Fight your phobia — and win*, Behavioural Press, London

Spielberger, C.D. and Sarason, I.G. (eds) (1975–1982) *Stress and anxiety* (series, vols 1–8 incl.), John Wiley & Sons, New York and Chichester

Strongman, K.T. (1978) *The psychology of emotion*, John Wiley & Sons, New York and Chichester

Truax, C.R. and Carkhuff, R.R. (1967) *Towards effective counselling and psychotherapy*, Aldine, Chicago

Vigersky, R. (1977) *Anorexia nervosa*, Raven Press, New York

# Index